S0-BDM-244

THE SURVIVAL GUIDE FOR

Money Smarts

EARN, SAVE, SPEND, GIVE

Eric Braun and Sandy Donovan

free spirit
PUBLISHING®

Library of Congress Cataloging-in-Publication Data
Names: Braun, Eric, 1971– author. | Donovan, Sandra, 1967– author.
Title: The survival guide for money smarts : earn, save, spend, give / Eric Braun and
    Sandy Donovan.
Description: Golden Valley, MN : Free Spirit Publishing Inc., [2016] | Includes index.
Identifiers: LCCN 2016019320 (print) | LCCN 2016029861 (ebook) | ISBN 9781631980282 (pbk.)
    | ISBN 1631980289 (pbk.) | ISBN 9781631981159 (Web pdf) | ISBN 9781631981166 (epub)
Subjects: LCSH: Finance, Personal—Juvenile literature. | Children—Finance, Personal—
    Juvenile literature.
Classification: LCC HG179 .B7256 2016 (print) | LCC HG179 (ebook) | DDC 332.024—dc23
LC record available at https://lccn.loc.gov/2016019320

Reading Level Grades 7 & Up; Interest Level Ages 9–14;
Fountas & Pinnell Guided Reading Level Z

Edited by Kimberly Feltes Taylor
Cover and interior design by Emily Dyer
Illustrations by Steve Mark

Additional graphics: currency icons p.2 © Eduard Kachan | Dreamstime.com; currency patterns used throughout book © Jslavy | Dreamstime.com and © Teenbull | Dreamstime.com

10 9 8 7 6 5 4 3 2 1
Printed in the United States of America
V20300716

Free Spirit Publishing Inc.
6325 Sandburg Road, Suite 100
Minneapolis, MN 55427-3674
(612) 338-2068
help4kids@freespirit.com
www.freespirit.com

Contents

Reproducible Forms

You can download and print these forms at
www.freespirit.com/money-smarts-forms.
Use password **4goals**.

Introduction
Raising Your Money IQ

There's something about money that makes people act totally weird. For example, we heard about a person who paid $24,300 for a suit of armor . . . for his guinea pig. Somebody else bought a $95,000 truffle. In case you didn't know, a truffle is a fungus, kind of like a mushroom. This truffle was a very special kind. Only highly trained dogs could find it. Still, could a fungus *really* be worth that much money?

Most of us can't afford costly truffles, or armor for our guinea pigs. But we still find plenty of ways to make silly choices with our money. We buy brand names when cheaper versions are just as good. We buy a video game and then quit playing it after a week. We buy the large popcorn at the movies (the sign *says* it's the best deal!) even though we'll never make it halfway through that grocery bag of popcorn. Many of us don't plan ahead or save enough.

Money, Money, Money

Different countries use different kinds of money, or **currency**. The United States and Canada use dollars, and that's the term we use in this book. If people use a different currency where you live, just think of that currency when you see the word "dollar" or the dollar sign ($ or $).

EURO

BRITISH POUND

SOUTH KOREAN WON

UNITED STATES DOLLAR

NIGERIAN NAIRA

JAPANESE YEN

INDIAN RUPEE

CURRENCY: the type of money used in a specific country

Maybe you don't make silly money choices. Maybe you've already got a savings account and some pretty sharp money smarts. If so, that's great! Or maybe you don't have much money and aren't sure how to get it. Maybe you've just never given money much thought. Whatever the case may be for you, this book can help you raise your money IQ. ("IQ" stands for "intelligence quotient." That's just a fancy way of saying how smart you are about something.)

To raise your money IQ, you'll start by thinking about your goals. Then you'll consider ways you can earn money to reach those goals. You'll also learn how to set up a budget that will help you manage your money. (Think a budget sounds scary or boring? Don't worry—a budget just means making a plan for your money.) Even though you may be too young to do things like work a "real" job, use a credit card, or invest in stocks, you'll learn about these things, too. Looking to the future, when you *can* do these things, is an important part of being money smart—and happy.

Warning! Having money smarts can lead to feelings of confidence, wisdom, and pride. That's because being money smart is all about making decisions that say something positive about you and the things you care about.

About This Book

This book has a *ton* of information. It covers everything from making money to saving and investing it . . . and a lot more. You'll get the most out of this book if you start from the beginning and read it all the way through. Then you can go back and reread anything you need a refresher about. Or, if you have something in mind right now that you want to learn about, you can check out the table of contents or the index to find it. For example, if you want to learn about ways to earn money, you can turn to Chapter 3 on page 24. Or if you get a job babysitting and want some tips for not wasting the money you make, you can turn to page 54 and read about budgets. And throughout the book, you'll see some forms that can help you boost your money smarts and practice the skills you'll be learning. You'll also find charts you can fill out to help you set your goals, create a budget, and manage your money. You can photocopy these pages from the book or download and print out copies. See page v for how to download the forms.

You'll also find lots of stories in this book that will help explain things and give examples of money smarts in action. **Real-World Kids** stories are about kids your age who have done really cool things. (The things they've done are amazing, but they're not so super-amazing that they're out of reach for you. Think of these kids as role models. You can do amazing things, too.) There are also **Money Smarts Stories**. These stories are about fictional kids who made *financial* mistakes but learned to make smarter choices.

FINANCIAL: having to do with money

Finally, you'll find **Choose Your Own Spending Ending** stories. These stories star *you* as the main character. You'll decide between two ways of using your money. After you choose, you'll have a chance later in the chapter to read what happens to you as a result of your decision. Be careful not to make a choice you'll regret! (Okay, okay, these things won't *really* happen to you. But the two endings are a fun way to look at different ways your choices can affect your life.)

You'll also see vocabulary boxes for important money words and phrases—like the ones you've already seen for the words *currency* and *financial*.

We hope *The Survival Guide to Money Smarts* will help you feel confident about your future and take some of the mystery out of money. We also hope it will be fun, because we don't think learning about money has to be a big bore. Instead, learning about money should be exciting. It might even be more exciting than a guinea pig in armor!

After you read this book, tell us how it helped you. If you have suggestions for making it better, we'd love to hear those, too. You can send us a letter at:

c/o Free Spirit Publishing
6325 Sandburg Road, Suite 100
Minneapolis, MN 55427-3674

Or you can email us at:
help4kids@freespirit.com.

Happy saving and spending!

Eric Braun
Sandy Donovan

1 Revenge of the Sandwich
(What Is Money, Anyway?)

Let's say you and your friends want to rent a movie, *Revenge of the Sandwich.* You get permission from your mom,* find the movie online, and click the remote to pay the $2.99 rental fee. (You'll pay your mom back later, of course.) Pop the popcorn and pass the fizzy drinks, because you and your buddies are in business.

. . . .

*When you see *mom* or *parent* or similar names in this book, think of whoever takes care of you. That may be your mom or dad, or it could be another adult like a foster parent, a grand-parent, an aunt, or an uncle.

Friends, couch, movie—that's a recipe for a great afternoon. But what about that $2.99? Why did you have to pay that? Where did it go? And should you even care? (*Hint:* This book is all about money, so the answer is probably *not* going to be, "No, you shouldn't care at all.")

Think about where that movie came from. *Revenge of the Sandwich* didn't just happen. Somebody had to write it. Somebody had to direct it. Making a movie takes actors, camera operators, costumes and costume designers, sets and set designers, stage crews, makeup artists, and . . . well, you get the point. For a lot of people, making that movie was their job. Your $2.99 is one tiny part of how all those people make their living and earn money to pay for their food, homes, and more.

Money = A Form of Exchange

Imagine what it would be like if we didn't have money. We would have to pay one another in some other way, such as by *exchanging*—or trading—goods or skills. For example, think about a person who knows how to fix computers. She can solve *anybody's* computer problems lickety-split. Which is great—but she also needs to eat. In a world with no money, how does she get food? She's great with computers, but she doesn't know anything about growing food. Heck, she doesn't have time to even *think* about it! She could always trade for food. For instance, maybe she can find a chicken farmer who has a broken computer. She could fix the farmer's computer in exchange for some eggs. Pretty simple, right? But what if she also wants some orange juice, toast, butter—and oh,

EXCHANGE: to trade one thing for another (such as money for goods)

maybe some new shoes? This trading could get pretty complicated pretty fast.

For another example, imagine you want a couple of granola bars. What do you have to offer in exchange? Maybe you could mow someone's lawn in exchange for them. But what if the person making the granola bars doesn't have a lawn? Or what if he doesn't need it mowed? Now you've got a problem.

People invented money to solve these kinds of problems. Today, people all over the world use money to buy and sell things, because *money is a form of exchange.* That means we all agree that it's worth something—and we can exchange it for goods and services that are worth the same amount. If we didn't have a system for agreeing on that worth, money would not have any value at all. It would just be paper and coins and numbers and symbols. So now when you want a granola bar, you don't have to trade lawn care with a granola bar maker. Instead, you trade money.

Money = Stored Value

In addition to being a form of exchange, *money stores value.* That means you can use it in lots of different ways. You can also save it and spend it later.

Imagine that you have a job scooping ice cream at an ice cream shop. If money didn't exist, the shop owner might have to pay you in scoops. That would be terrible! All your work would be for nothing but ice cream: Day after day, barrels of ice cream filling up your home. (Okay, maybe it would be fun for a while!)

But eventually your freezer would fill up. Your ice cream would melt. And you would get tired of ice cream (probably). You'd want to earn other things for your work. Maybe you'd want to buy clothes or music or a volleyball. Maybe you'd want to save up for something big.

Since you are paid in money, not ice cream, you have that freedom. You can spend your money how you want to. And you can save it for the future. (This is a GREAT idea and something we'll talk about a lot more later on in this book.) Unlike those barrels of ice cream, money never melts.

Money = Labor

Finally, *money is a measure of labor*. In other words, money represents our work.

Let's say you babysit a neighbor's kids for four hours. Your neighbor pays you $5 an hour, so after four hours of babysitting she gives you $20. Now you have $20 in your pocket—woo hoo! But before you run out and spend it on a new T-shirt, think: $20 equals four hours of your time. Is that T-shirt worth four hours of your time?

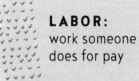

LABOR: work someone does for pay

Why Is Money Important?

Money is important because it makes it easy to buy, sell, and do things:

- **Money lets us buy things we need,** like food, and enjoy things we want, like renting *Revenge of the Sandwich.* We can buy small things and we can save up to buy big things.

- **Money keeps us safe.** We use it to pay for shelter and clothing. We pay money to the government for services like fire departments and police departments. And when we save money, we are taking care of our future selves.

- **Money also lets us help others.** We can *donate* money to organizations that will use it to help animals or people in need or to protect the earth. Or we can use our money to help family members or other people in our community.

What all this means is that money has power. We can use it in many, many different ways. So what will you choose to do with your money? Your answer says a lot about you. That's what the next chapter is about.

DONATE:
to give money
to a good cause

Who Are You?
(And What Do You Want?)

Being smart about your money is all about being responsible. It's about having a plan, making good decisions, and thinking about the future.

But hold on! If your eyes glaze over when you hear words like *responsible,* don't fall asleep. And don't toss this book out the window and run away screaming, "I don't need any more responsibilities in my life!" Because being smart about your money starts with something you might find pretty fun.

It starts with thinking about your goals—all the things you *want* in life.

That's right. Being money smart can help you reach your goals. And just what is a goal? A goal is something you want

SECURE: feeling safe, sure of yourself, and confident about the future

to achieve or have in the future. Reaching your goals can make you feel happy and *secure*.

Sometimes goals are objects you want to buy. Sometimes they are things you want to do. Some goals are small, and some are much bigger. Whatever your goals may be, they say a lot about who you are as a person.

Consider two sixth graders: Kiyari and Alex. Kiyari has the following goals:

- buy an electric guitar
- take guitar lessons
- start a band

Alex has these goals:

- buy a new softball glove
- make the highest-level softball team as a pitcher
- get a softball scholarship for college

Both kids have something they want to buy for themselves soon. For Kiyari, it's a guitar. For Alex, it's a new glove. Both kids want to do something that interests them. Kiyari wants to learn to play the guitar and start a band, while Alex wants to play high-level softball. Alex plans to go to college—so she's thought more about her future than Kiyari has. Maybe Kiyari just hasn't thought that far ahead yet. That's fine, of course. These kids are in sixth grade. People don't have to have their futures planned out in sixth grade. Even Alex might change her mind about softball in a few years.

The point is, you get a pretty good idea of who these two are by looking at their goals. Now it's time to look at your own goals—and find out more about yourself.

Brainstorm Your Goals

If you've never thought about your goals, that's okay. Many kids haven't. Or if you can't stop thinking about the gazillion things you need or want, that's okay too. Either way, it helps to make a list.

So copy or print out the "Brainstorm and Rate Your Goals" chart on page 22, or use pen and paper or a computer to list some ideas first. Don't be shy, and don't be worried you're going to make a mistake (you're not). Just write down the things that pop into your head when you think about your future.

Keep in mind that this list is just for financial goals— goals you need money to reach. Other kinds of goals are important, too, but being money smart won't necessarily help you with them.

You can also leave off small or short-term goals like buying a sports drink after school. You might have goals like that, but for this activity, you want to focus on things you have to plan and save up for (at least a little).

Think about goals that might fit into each of the following three categories:

1. **Short-term goals.** These are things you want to accomplish fairly soon, like in the next month. Examples are buying art supplies, going to the movies next weekend, or getting ingredients for baking cupcakes with friends. Slightly bigger (but still short-term) examples include throwing a holiday party, going to a theme park, or donating pet supplies to an animal shelter.

2. **Long-term goals.** These are things you want to make happen in the next year or so. Examples might be going to summer camp, buying a bike or skateboard, taking a dance class, or donating $100 to a children's hospital.

3. **Really long-term goals.** These goals are way out in the future—things you hope to do when you're older—like buying a car or house, traveling somewhere awesome, going to college, or starting a business.

Don't worry if your list seems too short or too long, or if it seems like you have too many short-term goals and not enough long-term ones. For now, think of your list as a starting point. You can add to it and subtract from it as you need to.

It's smart to think about your goals, even if they will change over time. Your goals might lead you somewhere unexpectedly great.

REAL-WORLD KID

Lizzie Marie Likness

When Lizzie Marie Likness was in elementary school, she had a goal. She wanted to take horseback riding lessons. To raise money for lessons, she baked healthy snacks and sold them at a local farmer's market. Things really took off from there. She and her dad built a website where she posted cooking videos. She started teaching healthy cooking classes in her community.

Soon Lizzie had a new goal. She wanted to teach others about how to cook and enjoy healthy food. By age 13, she had appeared on the *Rachael Ray Show* and starred in her own WebMD video series, *Healthy Cooking with Chef Lizzie*. Lizzie had met her first goal of earning money for horseback riding lessons—and she also met her new goal of spreading the word about healthy food.

Score Your Goals

The next step is to start thinking about how important each goal is to you. To help you do that, think about the following questions and give each category a score from 0 to 3 points.

> 0 = not at all
> 1 = a little
> 2 = a lot
> 3 = a whole lot

- **How happy will you be if you reach this goal?** Will you want to jump up and down with excitement? Or will it barely make you smile?

- **How proud will you be if you reach this goal?** Will you feel really good about yourself? Will you feel more confident? Could you feel bad about it for any reason?

- **How good will you feel about this goal five years after reaching it?** It might be hard to tell right now, but try to look ahead. Will you still be thinking about this goal? Or will it be long forgotten? Not all goals have to still be important to you in the future, but it helps to think about them this way. If achieving a goal will make you feel happy or proud for a long time, that goal might be extra important.

Here's an example of one girl's goals and her reasons for how she rated them. (See page 22 for a blank version of the chart that you can copy or print out and use for scoring your own goals.)

Money Smarts Story ▶ Shawna's Goals

Goal	How happy?	How proud?	How good 5 years later?	Total score
Buy frozen pizza for a sleepover this weekend	1	1	0	2
Get an app for making stop-motion movies	2	1	0	3
Take a stop-motion class at the community center	3	2	2	7
Get my dad a special chess set for his birthday	3	2	1	6
Fly to Cincinnati to visit my friend Camilla (Dad says he'll share the cost with me)	3	2	3	8

Shawna says:

Here's what I was thinking when I scored these goals. The sleepover will be really fun no matter what, but it's extra fun to have pizza at a party. It might make me a little proud to treat my friends to pizza, but five years from now I probably won't remember that night. I know I'll be happy about getting the stop-motion app because I've been wanting it for a long time. But I also have a free one I can use in the meantime, so it's not like it's the most important thing. It won't make me proud, exactly, and in five years there will be new apps anyway, so it won't matter to me then. On the other hand, taking the class will be super awesome, and I hope to learn skills that will last me a long time—at *least* five years.

My dad is really into chess, and we play together a lot. It will make him happy to get the chess set from me, and that will make me happy, too. I'll also feel proud of myself for getting him something that he really likes. If he still has it in five years, I bet that'll feel great.

The last goal is really important to me. My best friend Camilla moved away last summer. I have missed her SO MUCH! Even though we text practically all the time, I really want to see her. I think we'll be friends for a long time, so in five years I'll still feel great about this trip. Gotta make it happen!

Prioritize Your Goals

After you've scored all your goals, it's time to *prioritize* your list. To do that, list your goals in order of most points to fewest. Put short-term goals, long-term goals, and really long-term goals all on one list. Here's what Shawna's ordered list looks like:

PRIORITIZE: to rank things in order of importance

Goal	Total score
Fly to Cincinnati to visit Camilla (Dad says he'll share the cost with me)	8
Take a stop-motion class at the community center	7
Get my dad a special chess set for his birthday	6
Get an app for making stop-motion movies	3
Buy frozen pizza for a sleepover this weekend	2

Okay, do you have your list of goals? Are they arranged in order of priority? (See page 23 for a blank version of the chart you can copy or print and use for prioritizing your goals.) Remember, you can change this list any time, so don't feel pressured to get it exactly right. In fact, your list probably *will* change over time. The main point is to start thinking about your goals.

Think About Cost

Now ask yourself one more question:

How much will it cost to achieve each goal?

And how will that cost affect your other goals? Maybe Shawna gets an allowance and can save it for three weeks and buy pizza for all her friends at the sleepover. But what if she saved that money for her plane ticket to Cincinnati—a goal that is a lot more important to her? Long-term goals are usually more expensive, but they're also usually more important to us. That doesn't mean you should never treat yourself or try to complete short-term goals. It just means that you need to think about the cost of your goals and make that part of your prioritizing.

Later in this book, you'll make a plan for reaching your goals. As you start thinking about this, you might find that you can't reach every single goal. You'll have to decide which goals to cut from your list. The ones to cut are the ones at the bottom of your list—the goals that are least important to you.

Talk with Others

Everyone has different goals and different *values*. Your goals will be different from those of your friends, and your family's goals will be different from other families' goals. When you talk about goals and values with your friends and family, you understand them better, and they understand

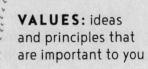

VALUES: ideas and principles that are important to you

you better. You might learn to see things in new ways. You might even develop new goals based on what you learn.

To start, ask your parent or parents what their goals were when they were your age. What was the toy, snack, or article of clothing they desperately wanted when they were kids? How much did those things cost? Were they able to save for them? How did they earn and save the money for them? How did their goals change as they got older?

Talk about the goals your family has now, too. What do the adults in your family hope the future will look like for all of you? Ask your parents if they are willing to talk with you about financial issues. How do they make financial decisions, such as whether to spend money on helping a relative, buying a TV, or going camping? How much—if any—*debt* does the family have? (Some adults prefer to keep this information private. If your family doesn't want to talk about debt, it's important to respect their privacy.)

Ask your friends what their goals are, too. You might learn about goals you never would have thought of on your own. Maybe one of your friends' goals will be so interesting that you'll decide to make it one of your goals, too.

DEBT: money owed to a person or an institution, such as a bank

Now What?

So, you've made a list of your goals and prioritized it. Great! Now it's time to wave your magic wand and *poof* . . . oh, wait. That's not the way it works. You're on your way to money smarts, but you're not there yet. The next step is to earn money. That's what Chapter 3 is about.

Brainstorm and Rate Your Goals

Brainstorm your goals and write them in the first column. In the next three columns, answer the questions by giving each goal a score from 0 to 3 points. Finally, add up the scores for each row and write the total in the last column. (See page 16 for an example of how to complete this chart.)

0 = not at all   1 = a little   2 = a lot   3 = a whole lot

Goal	How happy?	How proud?	How good 5 years later?	Total score

After completing this chart, use the "Prioritize Your Goals" chart on page 23 to put your goals in order of importance.

Prioritize Your Goals

Take a look back at the goals you identified on the "Brainstorm and Rate Your Goals" chart. Now prioritize them by listing your goals in order of most points to fewest. (See page 18 for an example of how to complete this chart.)

Goal	Total score

After completing this chart, hold on to it. Look at it before you spend money. It will help you remember what's really important to you and how you really want to use your money. Remember, this list can—and should—change. Cross off goals after you've reached them or if you decide they aren't right for you anymore. Add new ones as you think of them.

3 Beyond the Lemonade Stand
(Ways to Make Money)

Now that you have set some goals, all you need is the money to make them happen. Easy, right? Just ask your parents for cash. Better yet, ask your grandparents and aunts and uncles to kick in some dough, too. You'll have a nice pile in no time at all.

You know getting money is not that simple. That's why you're reading this book!

Getting an Allowance

Some kids get an *allowance*. That means their parents give them a set amount of money every week or every month. Some kids do certain chores in exchange for their allowance. Other kids receive an allowance without having to do anything specific.

ALLOWANCE: an amount of money given to someone on a regular basis

If you don't get an allowance, maybe your parents will be willing to give you one if you ask. But before asking for an allowance, think about whether your parents can afford to give you money. If they can't, skip to the next section to find out how you can earn money. If you think your parents may be able to afford it, then ask them—at the right time and in the right way. That means:

- Wait until your parents are relaxed and in a good mood.
- Be polite and *ask* for an allowance. Do not demand one. (For more on this, see "The Art of the Ask" on page 28.)
- Point out that getting an allowance will help you learn how to manage money.
- Explain that you will set a budget (see Chapter 4) and be responsible with your allowance money.
- Thank your parents at the end of the conversation— even if they do not agree to give you an allowance.

Many kids who receive an allowance get $5 to $10 a week. Some kids get more. If your parents agree to give you an allowance, they will have less money to spend on what they need and want. So be happy with any amount your parents are willing to give you. (And be understanding if your parents say no.)

Even if you already get an allowance, you might want to earn more money. People usually earn money in exchange for doing work. You may have heard of this—it's called having a job. Now, if you're thinking, "But I'm just a kid! I can't get a job!"—you might be right. Kids under the age of 14 usually can't get a real job in the United States or Canada. But if you think that means kids can't work to earn money, think again. Kids can earn money in plenty of ways. Here are a few that we'll discuss in this book:

- Ask your parents if they'll pay you to do some jobs at home
- Offer to do chores for friends and neighbors
- Sell things online or at garage sales

Any or all of these may be an option for you. Read on to learn more about each idea.

Helping Out at Home

For some kids, helping out at home is the best way to earn cash. They make money by doing extra chores and jobs.

The key to getting paid for extra chores is the word *extra*. It means you are doing more than your family already expects you to do. Most kids have certain chores they have to do at home. Maybe you have to keep your room clean, pick up your books and toys after you use them, and clear your dishes after a meal. You might get paid an allowance for doing these things, or you might not. Or you might get an allowance that has nothing to do with chores—you just get it for being a part of the family.

Whatever your situation is, it's important that you keep doing what your family expects of you. Asking to be paid for making your bed, which you're supposed to do anyway, is a good way to annoy a parent.

Chores You Can Do for Extra Money

Here are some ways kids make money at home. Some will be good ideas for you, while others will not. It depends on your age, where you live, whether you have pets, what your parents are willing to pay for, and other factors.

- Babysit a younger sibling
- Clean litter box or change out kitty litter
- Clean the bathroom—mirror, sink, tub, floor, and (yep) toilet
- Wash or fold laundry
- Empty the dishwasher
- Feed pets
- Make a meal
- Mow the lawn
- Pull weeds
- Take out trash and recycling
- Vacuum
- Walk the dog or pick up dog poop
- Wash dishes
- Water plants

Choosing Chores and Jobs

You can do two different kinds of tasks to earn money: repeated chores and one-time jobs. Repeated chores are a great option because you do them over and over—and get paid over and over, too. You don't repeat these chores because you keep doing a bad job. You repeat them because they keep getting undone.

Washing dishes is a chore like that. Say you wash the dishes tonight. Someone is going to have to wash them again the next time your family uses dishes (probably tomorrow at breakfast). If you dust the furniture in the living room, it will be dusty again in about a week.

One-time jobs are different. These are things like painting a chair, hanging a new shower curtain, or organizing the garage. You won't get paid over and over for these jobs. But since they are often a lot more work than regular chores, you can charge more for doing them. Maybe every time you go to the car your dad grumbles, "I really need to organize this garage, it's such a disaster." But he never seems to have the time to do it. That's your chance! Your dad might be willing to pay you to clean the garage for him.

Look for one or more repeated chores to keep the money coming in every week. And be an even smarter moneymaker by keeping an eye out for one-time jobs that can bring in some truly *extra* cash.

The Art of the Ask

How can you get a family adult to pay you for work? Like many things in life, it's all about communication. You can't just start doing any old chores and demand money. You'll have to talk to your parents or guardians first. This talk will go best if you're prepared. To start thinking about how to prepare, put yourself in the following story.

Choose Your Own Spending Ending

Can I Have a Job?

It's breakfast on a school day, and as usual, things are pretty hectic. Your dad is trying to pack up for work and clean up the kitchen at the same time. He's also helping your little brother Dexter get ready for first grade. Halfway through a bite of his waffle, Dexter suddenly says, "I just remembered! I need you to sign a permission slip for my field trip tomorrow." Your dad groans and says, "Where is it?"

As the two of them scramble around looking for the form, you finish up your waffles. You check the clock on the oven and see that you have seven minutes before you have to start walking to school. Since your backpack is all ready, you can take your time. No stress for you!

Then you remember that you meant to ask your dad if you could start doing extra chores for money.

> ## What do you do?

1 > You say to your dad, "I was thinking you should start paying me for cleaning up my dishes after breakfast. That way I would do it more often." ***Turn to* Ending 1** *on page 32.*

. . . .

2 > You clean up your breakfast dishes *and* put away the butter, milk, and syrup. *And* you get a rag to wipe up your own spot as well as Dexter's. *And* you remind your dad that you saw Dexter's field trip form on the couch. That night, when things are calm and your dad is relaxed, you say, "Dad, I've been thinking. I'd really like to earn a little extra money by helping out at home. I notice that you get pretty busy in the mornings, so maybe I could make breakfast and pack lunches. That way you'd have more time to get ready and be on time for work. Do you think you'd be able to pay me a little to do that? Or maybe there's another way I could help out and earn some money?" ***Turn to* Ending 2** *on page 32.*

. . . .

You don't have to be a financial genius to figure out which of these scenarios is going to work better, do you? But before you skip ahead and read the spending endings, check out the following list of three important questions. These are things to think about before asking parents for extra paid work.

3 Questions to Consider When Asking Adults for Money to Do Chores

1. **Does your family have the money to pay you for chores?** This is key. If there's simply no extra money in your household, then there's no point in asking. That doesn't mean you can't earn money! It just means you're going to have to try another method. Take a look at the next section, "Working for Friends and Neighbors," on page 37.

2. **Do you have a good idea of the kinds of chores you could do?** It's always smart to have specific ideas for chores you could do. That means *helpful* chores, so don't ask your mom to pay you for cleaning out the "extra" ice cream in the freezer. Instead, consider what the adult might think of the chores. The chores you suggest should be tasks you can actually handle on your own. They should also be tasks that your parents might really want to have done. Are there certain things your parents always seem to complain about but don't have the time or energy to deal with? Put them on the list.

3. **Is this a good time to ask?** Asking at a bad time means you're less likely to get a "yes." The right time to ask is when the people you're asking are in a good mood and have enough time to think about it. It's also good to ask when you've recently shown that you are dependable or just an all-around good kid.

So how will your spending ending go? Let's take a look.

See Your Spending Ending

Can I Have a Job?

Ending 1

Your dad looks at you for a second before replying. His hair and clothes are messed up from searching for the permission slip. And he has syrup dripping off his fingers. *Great timing!* you think. *He really needs my help, so he'll for sure say yes.*

"Sure," your dad says. "I'll pay you to clean up your own breakfast. Do you want me to pay you to go to school, too? How about if I pay you $50 every time you go to the bathroom? You deserve it!"

"Uh," you say, not sure what he means. "Are you serious?"

"No!" your dad says, signing Dexter's field trip form with sticky fingers. "I'm not serious. We don't pay kids for doing what is already expected of them. Now clean up your dishes and go to school."

The End

Ending 2

Your dad looks at you for a second before replying. "That sounds like a good idea," he finally says. "There are probably a *lot* of ways you could help out around here, not just at breakfast."

"Yeah," you say. "I was thinking I could clean the gecko cage every month, too. I know you hate that job."

"Good idea," Dad says. "But it's almost time for bed. So let's talk more about it this weekend!"

The End

If you chose Ending 2, good for you! You chose wisely.

Of course, asking the right way doesn't guarantee success. You might ask about doing chores for money and your parent might be totally against the idea. If so, you will have to move on to other options. Some families just don't pay for doing chores. If that's the case, you're probably not going to change it.

On the other hand, maybe your family is a little nervous about giving you the job. Maybe they're not sure you can handle it. If so, find out what part concerns them. For example . . .

What if they think you don't know how to do the job, or won't do a good job?

If you know how to do the chore you have in mind, tell them the steps you'll take to complete it. That way, they'll know you can do it. If you aren't sure about how to do the chore, be honest. Then ask them to teach you.

What if they're worried you won't follow through?

Show them that you're serious about doing the job. Tell them exactly *when* you plan to do the chore. Tell them how much time it will take. Details like this can let adults know that you're not just throwing ideas out there—you have thought things through.

What if they're afraid you won't have time for your homework or other responsibilities on top of extra chores?

Again, showing that you've thought it out can ease their concerns. Tell them exactly *when* and *how* you will fit all your responsibilities into your day.

A trial period might be a good way to test things out. Maybe you will walk the dog every day after school for two weeks. After two weeks, check in with the family to see how you did. If you had to be reminded a bunch of times and skipped it a few days, your mom might tell you that you failed the trial period. But if you did the job every day with no reminders—and no complaining!—your mom will probably be willing to pay you for that job. Remember, it's up to you to show that you're responsible enough to get the job done.

Whatever you do, don't give your new employer any reason to doubt you. Do the job on time and do it thoroughly. (So if you're doing the dishes, don't leave the frying pan for someone else to wash. Or if you're mowing the lawn, mow the *whole* lawn. Don't leave any patches—even small ones—unmowed.) And do it with a smile. You don't want to mess up any future opportunities by blowing your first chance.

Brothers and Sisters

Never overlook the value of older siblings when it comes to earning money. If you're lucky enough to have siblings or other older teens in your life, there's a good chance that they have a small income. There's an even better chance they have some chores they'd rather not do. Maybe they want to get out of their weekly table-setting duties. Or they hate having to fold the laundry and put it away. Too bad for them . . . but too *good* for you. This is your chance to step in and kindly offer to take over their chore—for a small fee, of course. (Check with your parents, too. Make sure they are okay with you doing the chore.)

How Much Should You Charge?

Your *fee*—what you charge for your work—isn't something you get to decide on your own. Instead, it's something you and your family have to agree on. If you ask for 50 bucks to vacuum the living room, guess what? You're going to be paid zero bucks, because no parent is going to agree to that.

FEE: a payment for a service

So how do you set a fee for a chore? First, think about what seems fair. Here are some things to consider:

- Do you get an allowance already? If you do, and if you do chores for that allowance, you probably have some idea of what your family is willing to pay for chores. Compare the new chore to the ones you already do. Is it harder or easier? More time-consuming? Is it grosser?

- How long will the chore take? You deserve more money for chores that take longer.

- What can your family afford? Ask your parents how much they think they can pay you if you take on extra chores.

- How much do you need to make in order to feel good about the chore? In other words, if cleaning the toilet makes you feel grumpy every single time you do it, then you should ask for more for that chore. (Or choose a different chore.)

- How pleasant—or *un*pleasant—is the chore? Those awful, terrible, disgusting, or painful chores that nobody wants to do might pay a little more. Picking up dog poop probably deserves more pay than folding a load of laundry.

After coming up with what you think is a fair fee, suggest it to your parent. If you're asking for too much, your mom or dad will let you know. Together you can figure out a rate that works for everyone.

Often, the parent will be the one to suggest the rate. In that case, it's okay to ask for a little more if you really think it would be more fair—but be respectful. Think about the factors listed on page 35 and explain your reasons. Still, don't be surprised if your parent isn't ready to budge just yet. You might have to do a great job at the chore for a while, and then come back and ask for a raise.

Types of Payment for Work

You'll charge a fee for the jobs you do at home (or for your neighbors). When you get older, you might get an after-school or weekend job at a grocery store, restaurant, or other business. It will probably pay an hourly wage. You might already have a job like that now. As an adult, you might also have a job that pays an hourly wage. Or maybe you'll get a job that pays a salary. Here are some examples of different ways people get paid for work:

- **Fee:** a set amount paid for a specific task
  Example: *My fee for raking leaves is $8 a yard.*

- **Wage:** a set amount of pay, usually by the hour, for an ongoing job
  Example: *Ana earns a wage of $11 per hour as a cashier at the grocery store.*

- **Salary:** a set amount of pay for a whole year for an ongoing job (paid on a weekly or monthly basis)
  Example: *Ahmed earns a salary of $45,000 per year as an office manager.*

Working for Friends and Neighbors

Getting paid to do chores at home is a great way to earn some extra money—but it's not the only way. For some kids, the best bet is to do chores outside their homes.

What Services to Offer

Maybe you already know exactly what services you're going to offer. Dog walking? Grass mowing? Babysitting? If you already know—great!

Or maybe you just know that you want to work and make some money. If that's the case, think about what the people in your neighborhood might need or want done. Babysitting and pet care are often in demand. If you live in a neighborhood with lawns, yard care services like mowing, weeding, raking, and shoveling snow can be pretty popular, too. If you live in an apartment building, your neighbors might need help carrying groceries upstairs or taking care of their plants or pets.

How can you figure out what people in your community might be willing to hire you to do? Here are a few ideas:

- Look at help-wanted signs around your neighborhood
- Ask your parents if your neighborhood has a website for classified ads
- Ask your family and closest neighbors what kinds of services they think people could use or might want

Also consider your skills and interests. Suppose you learn that both babysitting and lawn care are needed in your neighborhood. And suppose that the thought of changing a diaper makes you shudder. If that's the case, you should probably go with lawn care. If possible, it's best to choose jobs that match with your experience, skills, and interests.

Advertising Your Business

Once you decide on the service to offer, it's time to *advertise*. You can advertise in three main ways.

ADVERTISE: to let people know about a product or business

Word of mouth. This means telling everyone you know to tell everyone they know about your business. You can tell your friends' parents. You can tell your neighbors if you happen to see them outside. Or you can knock on doors in your neighborhood to get the word out. (Check with your parent before doing this.) You can also ask a parent to tell the adults they know that you're looking for work.

Posters and flyers. Make posters and flyers that tell people about your business. Include the service you are offering, how much you will charge, and how to contact you. You can hang the posters on community bulletin boards in grocery stores, coffee shops, and community centers. (Ask an employee first.) You can put flyers under people's doors. You can also hand out flyers when you tell people about your business.

Online advertising. See if you can post an ad on a free online bulletin board for your neighborhood or town. Lots of neighborhood associations and local newspapers have these.

Since you're a kid, you're going to want a grown-up to approve your advertising plans. A grown-up can also help you reply to strangers who contact you about your business. And to be safe, always have an adult come with you to meet a new customer.

Advertising Yourself

When you're a businessperson—and you *are* one if you're offering services to earn money—you are not only selling your services. You are also always selling *yourself.* This means you want to show that you're responsible. So you'll probably want to start wearing a business suit every day. Just kidding! You don't need to pretend to be someone you're not. You just need to be someone people *want* to hire. That means you want to be sure to make a good impression on the grown-ups you meet. Those grown-ups might decide to hire you—if you seem responsible and friendly.

Think about ways you can show that you're someone neighbors can trust to do a good job. For instance, say you're in a huge hurry to get to your friend's place. You could shave about 30 seconds off your bike ride if you cut across the yard on the corner. Your neighbors will understand, right?

Well, maybe not. Those neighbors might find it rude that you treated their lawn like a bike path. It might not be safe if people are in the yard. And it might damage the grass. If you treat someone else's property with disrespect, can you really be trusted to work for them? Chances are your neighbors won't want to hire you to take care of their pets, children, or lawn anytime soon.

Not being rude or disrespectful is the least you can do. But you can do more than that. There are plenty of ways you can show you're a responsible kid. Looking people in the eye and replying to their questions with complete sentences—not just one-word answers—are good ways. Even a simple smile or "How are you today?" are super ways to impress an adult.

By impressing the adults (and kids) in your life, you are building your reputation—the way people think of you. And having a good reputation is a great way to get jobs. Take the time to think about how you want people to see you, and do what you can to leave the best possible impression on others.

Doing the Job

The actual work you do is the most important step in building your reputation. If you do a great job, people might tell others about your work. That can lead to more people wanting to hire you. If you do a poor job, though, people are even more likely to talk to others—and tell them how disappointed they were with your work.

If someone trusts you enough to do a job for him or her, don't let that person down. How can you make sure you leave a positive impression? Here are a few tried-and-true ways.

- **Show up on time.** Better yet, show up a little early!
- **Show up prepared to work.** That means bringing the supplies you'll need. If you've been hired to mow someone's lawn, don't show up without a lawn mower unless you worked it out ahead of time that you'll use the customer's mower. If you are babysitting for someone who will be out late, don't show up so tired that you can't stay awake.

- **Finish the job.** If you're pulling weeds for someone, don't leave until all the weeds are pulled. But what if your friends come by to let you know they're playing soccer down at the park, and you really want to join them? Finish the job anyway.

Selling Things for a Profit

Plenty of kids earn money by selling their services doing chores or neighborhood jobs. But you can also sell *things* to bring in some cash.

There are two main types of items you can sell:

- things you make
- things you already own

Notice that some things don't fall into either of those groups—like your family's couch, your big sister's clothes, or anything else that's not actually *yours* to sell. Never fear! That still leaves lots of options for your business.

Things you make can include food and drinks like cupcakes, cookies, or anything else you know how to whip up. (Just be sure to get an okay for whatever ingredients you plan on using from your family's kitchen—or buy your own.) You can also make and sell art projects, like things you knit, draw, or build. If you need inspiration or directions, check online and at the library for lots of good project ideas.

Other things you can sell include items you already own but no longer need. That can be toys, books, or other things you dig out from under your bed or the back of your closet. Just remember, if you're going to charge money for something, it needs to be in good, working condition. And it probably shouldn't be something you received as a gift since that could make the gift-giver feel bad. (So you probably shouldn't sell that *Big Book of Railroad Facts* your uncle gave you!) After finding things to sell, show them to your parents. Make sure they are okay with what you've chosen.

You can sell your items one of two ways. You can hold a sale or advertise on the Internet.

REAL-WORLD KIDS

Jaden Wheeler and Amaya Selmon

It started on a spring day when Jaden Wheeler and Amaya Selmon decided to sell sno-cones in their front yard in Memphis, Tennessee. They called their stand Kool Kidz Sno Konez. Running a blender connected to a long extension cord, the siblings sold sno-cones all summer long. They did well enough to return the following summer. This time they had a fancy "Kool Kidz Kart" and a real ice shaver.

Over those two summers, they earned about $1,000. For the following summer, they took a big step: They bought a truck (with help from their mom). The Kool Kidz Sno Konez truck is driven by their mom, but the business is operated by the kids. They serve 20 flavors of sno-cones, including Barack O'Bubblegum and Peace Out Pink Lemonade. They even added "Not Yo Nachos" and "Hot Diggity Dawgs" to their menu.

Holding a Sale

Holding a sale—like a garage sale, yard sale, or bake sale—can be a lot of fun. You get to meet people and talk about what you're selling. Your sale could be a one-hour event or a weekend-long extravaganza. Whatever you have in mind, follow the steps below to help it go as smoothly as possible. (See page 52 for a checklist you can use when holding your own sale.)

1. **Get permission from a parent or guardian.** This is the most important step. Consider this person your adult helper. Your adult helper will help you set up and will also be with you at the sale. You should check in with him or her about all of the following steps.

2. **Pick a location.** Maybe your location is going to be your own home, yard, or sidewalk. Or maybe you know of a spot where more people—potential customers!—might pass by, like a busy park. Either way, check with your adult helper about the location and make sure he or she is comfortable with it. Also work with your adult helper to make sure you follow all rules and laws when selling in a public place, even on your own sidewalk.

3. **Pick a date and time.** Weekends or evenings are usually best for sales. Most people aren't at work or school then, so they can stop by. A common garage sale time is on the weekend, starting early in the morning (7:30 or 8:00 a.m.) and lasting until early afternoon. At a cookie stand, you might have brisk business right after school.

4. **Find additional helpers.** Ask friends or family members if they can help out, as well. For example, if you're planning a yard or garage sale, you're probably going to need help setting up. You may also need help collecting money, keeping an eye on items, and cleaning up at the end. You can ask your helpers if they want to sell some items of their own, too.

5. **Advertise.** Make posters to hang in your neighborhood. Telephone poles at busy intersections are a good place to tack up or tape your signs. (Tip: Don't forget to take down the signs when the sale is over.) Also spread the word to family, friends, neighbors, and people at your school.

6. **Get change and make a plan for storing cash.** Most likely, you'll need to make change for your customers. Have coins as well as plenty of $1 and $5 bills. Use a small box or money belt for storing money during the sale. People do sometimes steal, even from kids. So every so often, have your adult helper put the money you've earned in a safe place such as his or her wallet or your home.

7. **Set up.** For garage sales or yard sales, do whatever setup you can the night before, because it could take some time. Place the things you're selling on clean tables. Make sure the items you're selling are clean and in good shape. Mark prices on your items with masking tape or stickers. If you're running a cookie stand or a similar type of business, you probably don't have to get ready so early. But you do want to make sure you have enough cookies or whatever it is you're planning to sell. And it's always a good idea to check in with your adult helper to make sure he or she agrees with your plans and pricing ideas.

8. **During your sale be friendly, polite, and responsible.** Give your customers your full attention. Answer their questions politely.

9. **At the end of the sale, clean everything up.** This is part of being responsible. If you do a great job cleaning up, adults are a lot more likely to give you permission and help the next time you want to have a sale.

10. **Count your money and relax.** Hopefully, you had a good time *and* made some money! And after working so hard,

don't waste your earnings. Put the money in your budget envelopes (see Chapter 4) or into your savings account (see Chapter 6).

Selling Online

You can also try selling things online at websites like eBay or Etsy. Your adult helper will have to be very involved if you choose this way to make money, because it's illegal for kids to sell things online on their own. Also, you'll need help taking items to the post office to mail to your buyers, since most of them probably won't live near you. And your buyers will pay electronically, over the Internet, rather than in cash. These electronic payments will go into your adult helper's bank account. Then your helper will give you the money.

So why would you sell online instead of holding a sale yourself? For one thing, it can be easier in some ways. You can fit it into your schedule, even if it's a few minutes a day, instead of having to block off a specific date and time. But mostly, people sell online because they can reach a bigger group of customers. This is especially important if you're selling rare, unusual, or hard-to-find items.

Older, high-quality toys and games are great examples of these kinds of items. There are plenty of collectors who will pay good prices for complete toy sets or video games that aren't available in stores anymore. If you have some of these items and they're in good shape, talk to your adult helper about trying to sell them.

If you're a particularly artistic or crafty person, you may also want to consider selling some of your artwork or projects on Etsy or similar websites. Again, you'll have to talk it over with an adult helper and have him or her register and do the selling for you.

TAX FACTS

If you make enough money from selling things or providing services, you may have to pay *income tax* to the government. Depending on what you sell or the services you provide, you may also have to collect *sales tax* from your buyers and send the sales tax to your local or state government. Taxes can be complicated, so work with your adult helper to research tax laws in your area.

Even if you don't have to pay taxes now, it's good to know about what they are and how they work. When you're old enough to have a real job, you'll definitely have to pay taxes on the income you earn.

INCOME TAX: a percentage of your income that you must pay to the government

SALES TAX: a percentage of the price of a purchased item, which goes to the government

The government uses this money for many things such as roads, schools, police departments, fire departments, and hospitals.

Most likely, your employer will deduct the taxes from your pay and send it to the government for you. Here's how it works: You'll get paid every week, every two weeks, or every month. You might get a paper check or an electronic deposit directly into your bank account. You will also get a pay stub. Like the payment itself, it can be paper or electronic. The pay stub has lots of information on it, including:

- your name
- the dates that the check covers (the pay period)
- how many hours you worked
- your rate of pay
- how much you earned that period
- how much you paid in taxes
- other deductions

So if you worked for 20 hours at $8 per hour, you earned $160 (20 x 8). But your paycheck will not be for $160. Instead, it might be for $130, depending on how much you had to pay in taxes and other deductions.

In the United States, other deductions include payments to federal government programs like Social Security. Social Security pays money to retired people, people who are too sick to work, and others. Another of these programs is Medicare, which pays medical bills for people who have retired. Paying for these programs might seem like a bit of a bummer now, but they might help you someday in the future!

At the end of the year, workers add up how much they earned and how much they paid in taxes and other deductions. If they paid too much in taxes, they get a refund. If they didn't pay enough, they have to send more money to the government.

Making a Business Plan

When you plan to sell things or work for people outside your family, it's a good idea to make a plan for your business. A business plan helps you make smart business decisions, like how much to charge.

A business plan isn't complicated. You don't need a special app or a business degree. You can make your business plan by answering the following questions. Copy or print out the blank business plan outline on page 53 and use that, or write down your answers on a separate sheet of paper.

What's Your Idea?

What service will you offer, or what will you sell? Maybe you're doing lawn care or babysitting. Maybe you're selling homemade sculptures or sno-cones. (See page 37 for tips on picking a service, and check out pages 41–45 for ideas about what to sell.)

How Will You Advertise?

If people don't know about your business, they can't become customers. Get the word out! See page 38 for ideas.

What Are Your Expenses?

Whatever you decide to do, it will probably cost something to get your business up and running. Let's say you're going with a classic idea: a lemonade stand. In that case, you'll have to buy lemons and sugar. You will need to buy cups, and you might also have to buy a pitcher and a bag of ice. Some of your *expenses* might be one-time costs that you pay to start up. For example, you would probably only have to buy a lemonade pitcher one time. Other expenses will have to be paid over and over again. You'll need more lemons and sugar every time you make lemonade.

EXPENSES:
money you spend to run your business

If you're offering a service instead of selling things, you may still have expenses. Maybe you need to buy gloves and lawn bags for pulling weeds. Maybe you want to buy a game to play with the kids you babysit. If you walk dogs, you might have to buy poop bags and doggie treats. If you're selling items online, you probably have to buy packing supplies and pay for shipping.

You might have to pay something for your advertising, too. For example, if you make posters, do you have to buy paper and markers?

Make sure you write down *all* your expenses—one-time costs as well as ongoing costs.

What Is Your Cost Per Unit?

This is simply your total expenses divided by the number of jobs you do or items you sell. For example, how much does it cost you to walk one dog? Maybe it's one poop bag and two doggie treats. Or how much does it cost you to make one cup of lemonade?

Let's look at that lemonade stand example. Say your mom takes you to the grocery store and you buy lemons, sugar, cups, and a pitcher for a total of $9. You have ice and a cooler at home, so you don't need to buy them. Your pitcher holds 12 cups of lemonade, and with the supplies you bought, you can make 5 pitchers. That means your $9 pays for 60 cups of lemonade.

To find your cost per unit, divide $9 by 60:
$$\$9.00 \div 60 = 15¢$$

So it costs you 15 cents to make each cup of lemonade. And next time you run your lemonade stand, it will cost even less—because you already have the pitcher!

How Much Will I Sell It For?

Of course, you want to charge more for your product than it costs you to make it. If it costs 15 cents to make a cup of lemonade, don't charge 10 cents a cup. If you do, you're losing money. But if you charge too much, nobody will buy your lemonade. The key is to keep your price low enough that people will want to pay it, but high enough that it is worth all your costs as well as your time and trouble. The whole point of working or selling is to make a *profit*—more money than you spend.

To figure out what you should charge, you can do some research online or ask an adult for advice. Try to find that sweet spot where

PROFIT: money you make after expenses

you feel good about the money you're making *and* customers feel like they're getting a good deal. Everybody wins!

How Much Will I Make?

This is easy to figure out. Take the amount that you'll charge per unit and subtract your cost per unit. If you charge 50 cents for a cup of lemonade that costs you 15 cents to make, you're making 35 cents per cup. That might not sound like much. But remember, it's 35 cents for *every* cup. If you sell all 60 cups, you will earn $21. (That's $60 \times \$0.35 = \$21.00$.)

Here's an example business plan for Kyle.

Kyle's Business Plan

My idea: Raking leaves. We have lots of trees in my neighborhood, so in the fall that means one thing: lots of leaves. I kind of like raking, and I know a lot of people do *not*. Kyle to the rescue!

How I'll advertise: We have a neighborhood social website where people put up news and ads. My dad subscribes to it, so I asked if I could advertise using his profile. He said yes!

My expenses: We already have a rake, so I don't need to buy one. But I'm going to need a lot of lawn bags. I bought 35 for $13.

My cost per unit: I have homework and soccer practice after school, so I'll only rake on weekends. I plan to do four yards each of the next three weekends. That's 12 yards. My expenses are $13, so I divide $13.00 by 12, which equals about $1.08 per yard.

How much I will charge: From my experience raking our yard, I know it takes about an hour to rake an average yard. For a corner house, it probably takes about an hour and a half. I

asked my mom what she thinks, and she said professionals charge about $14 to $20 per yard in our neighborhood. So I decided that I'll charge $8 for a regular yard and $12 for a corner yard. That seems like a good deal for customers. And I'll feel great about earning that much for a couple hours of work.

How much I'll make: Out of the 12 yards, two are on corners. Ten regular yards at $8 each is $80, and two corner yards at $12 each is $24. That's a total of $104. Take out the $13 I spent on bags, and I will make $91 over the course of three weeks. Not bad!

Whether you earn money by doing chores around the house, doing chores for neighbors, or selling things, you are doing more than just earning money. You're also earning experience. You're learning how to be responsible and how to work with others. Plus, you're figuring out how to manage money. Managing money is what the next chapter is all about.

Holding a Sale: A Checklist

Follow these steps to organize and prepare for your sale. Check off each step as you complete it. (See pages 43–45 for more information about each step.)

☐ 1. **Get permission and help from a parent or guardian.**
     My adult helper is: _____

☐ 2. **Pick a location.**
     My sale will be at: _____

☐ 3. **Pick a date and time.**
     Date: _____
     Time: _____

☐ 4. **Find additional helpers.**
     My extra helpers are: _____
     _____
     _____

☐ 5. **Advertise.**
     ☐ I put up posters.
     ☐ I told family, friends, neighbors, and people at school.
     ☐ I took down the posters after the sale.

☐ 6. **Get change and make a plan for storing cash.**
     I will keep my cash in _____

☐ 7. **Set-up is complete.**
     ☐ I cleaned the items.
     ☐ I priced my items.
     ☐ My adult helper approved my prices.
     ☐ I know how and when I will set up.

☐ 8. **During your sale, be friendly, polite, and responsible.**

☐ 9. **At the end of the sale, clean everything up.**

☐ 10. **Count your money and relax!**

My Business Plan

Complete each of the following sections to create your business plan. (See pages 50–51 for an example of how to complete this outline.)

My idea: _____

_____

_____

How I'll advertise: _____

_____

_____

My expenses: _____

_____

_____

My cost per unit: _____

_____

_____

How much I will charge: _____

_____

_____

How much I'll make: _____

_____

_____

After creating your business plan, hold on to it. Update it as you change your idea (or have brand-new ideas), discover new costs, or decide to change how much you will charge. Remember, the goal is to make money! So make sure you charge enough to cover your costs and your time.

4

It's Time for a Plan
(Making a Budget)

So, your uncle paid you $8 to mow his lawn, and then you made $14 selling brownies—all in one day. You don't want to let that $22 sit around getting old and smelly, right? Better head over to the frozen yogurt shop. You deserve it after all that hard work. And hey, why not treat your friends, too? A round of fro-yo for everyone!

Uh, what's that? The bill for four heaping bowls of frozen yogurt is $21? Well, no problem. You are Ms. Money Bags, after all. Except all of a sudden, you're Ms. No Money. Oh well, being rich was fun while it lasted, right? What's the point of having money if you're not going to spend it?

You could look at it that way. Or you could look at it another way. Is it really worth spending most of your day earning money just to blow it all and be broke again an hour later? Most people would agree that's not a fun way to live. Sure, it's not so bad for a little while. But remember those goals you thought about when you read Chapter 2? (If you don't remember, or haven't read that chapter yet, check out pages 11–23.) You're not going to reach your goals if you spend all your money right after you make it.

This is where making a budget comes in. A budget is just a plan for keeping track of your money. Having a plan can help you make decisions about what to do with your money. It can keep you from going broke. And it can help you reach your goals.

Money In = Money Out

Making a budget isn't complicated. It's not like building a rocket or bringing about world peace. It's just one simple equation: Money in equals money out. So the money you earn (or get as gifts or an allowance) should equal the money you spend, *plus* the money you give away, *plus* the money you save for your goals.

You might have noticed something about that last sentence. It doesn't say, "The money you earn should equal the money you spend." Or, "The money you earn should equal the money you save for your goals." Nope. Look at it again:

> The money you earn should equal the money you spend, **plus** the money you give away, **plus** the money you save for your goals.

In other words, you don't spend ALL the money you earn. And you don't save ALL the money you earn. And, even if

CHARITY: an organization that raises money to help people, animals, or the environment, or to address other needs

you want to be the world's most generous philanthropist (that's a fancy word for a person who gives away money—usually to a *charity*—to help others), you don't donate ALL the money you earn. Instead, you have to come up with a plan for your money that includes all of those actions. It's a spending, saving, and donating plan.

Why Do People Donate to Charities?

People donate money to charities for all kinds of reasons. They want to help other people. They want to make the world a better place. They care deeply about certain issues. They want to feel good. Sometimes, people donate money for all of these reasons.

Which Budget Type Are You?

There's no one way to make an ideal budget. The right budget for one person might be the wrong budget for somebody else. Different people need different budgets for lots of reasons. People have different needs, which means they need to spend different amounts. They have different goals, which means they have to save different amounts. And of course they have different priorities and values.

But the bottom line is, everyone needs a plan for his or her money. And for most people, that plan includes spending, saving, and donating. Take a look at the following popular budget plans and see which one fits you best.

The 30-30-30-10 Plan

One of the most popular budgets around, this plan marks some money for spending, some for saving, and some for donating. The twist is that it lets you specifically track your short-term and your long-term goals. (Remember those? Short-term goals are the things you hope to buy or do soon. Long-term goals are further away, like a year or so out. And *really* long-term goals are way out in your future. Those are things like buying a car, going on a trip, or going to college.)

How does the 30-30-30-10 plan work? This budget breaks down your total income (or your "money in") like this:

- **30 percent** for spending or for family expenses
- **30 percent** for saving for short-term goals
- **30 percent** for saving for long-term and really long-term goals
- **10 percent** for donating to charity

Who is it best for? With its focus on saving for both short-term and long-term goals, this is obviously a plan for a serious planner. It's also a plan for a serious saver. With this budget, you're saving more than half (60 percent) of your total income. If you can make this work, it's a great way to get started on the road to meeting your goals. Later on, you'll feel great that you met your short-term, long-term, and really long-term goals. And if you stick to this plan, you won't have many moments of regret, like realizing you've just blown all of your hard-earned money in one short frozen-yogurt shop visit.

I love skateboarding. That's me in one word: *Skater*. My friends have been going to this laser tag place every Saturday for a few months now, and that's fun, but it costs 10 bucks every time you go. You can spend a couple hours there for 10 bucks, so my friends are like, "It's a good deal!" And it is, I guess, but I'm not as into it as they are. What *am* I into?

Skateboarding!

Just checking to see if you were paying attention. So I might go with my friends once a month or something, but I'm not going to do that every weekend. It's too much. Not when I'm saving up for new wheels for my skateboard since mine are getting thrashed. And not when I'm *also* saving up for surf lessons. My cousin surfs a lot, and she says I would love it. I can take lessons down at the beach when I visit her next summer. I'm going for it!

I added up the cost of the wheels and surf lessons, and I'll need to save about $200. That's a ton!

I don't get a big allowance, so saving $200 is not going to be easy. But I've been babysitting some little dudes on my block, and I tutored another dude in math. So I'm earning extra money where I can.

Plus, my dad told me about the 30–30–30–10 plan. I'm using it to help me reach my savings goals. I'm putting 30 percent toward saving for my new wheels, and I should have them pretty soon. I'm putting 30 percent toward the surf lessons, which I should be able to take when we visit my cousin next summer. Actually, I'll even have some money left over. I don't have any really long-term goals yet, but I'm saving the extra money for when I figure that out.

I'm also spending 30 percent on regular stuff like laser tag with the guys and the occasional orange-and-peanut-butter malt—totally the best!

Oh, and I put 10 percent toward this organization that protects the habitats of beach wildlife. I have fun at the beach. But I never forget that the beach is also home to all kinds of animals. And I never want them to lose their homes.

Meanwhile, I keep on skating!

The Three Thirds Plan

Sometimes called the 3-3 plan for short, the Three Thirds plan is for people who like to keep things simple. And it *is* simple: You take your total income ("money in") and divide it by 3.

How does the Three Thirds plan work? This budget has just three categories for your money:

- **one-third** for spending
- **one-third** for saving
- **one-third** for donating

Who is it best for? With one-third of your money going to donations, this is the budget for people who feel strongly about one or more causes.

Money Smarts Story ▶ Ella, Age 13
A Three Thirds Plan Fan

I love animals. Big ones, small ones, I love them all—but I love dogs the most. So I was really excited when I got to watch my neighbors' dogs, Violet and Penny, while my neighbors were on vacation. I loved feeding and playing with them, and it was *super* fun having the little pooches sleep in my room! I even liked getting up early to take them for walks.

Lucky for me, my neighbors are retired and go on lots of vacations. So I get to take care of Violet and Penny a lot. Plus, the neighbors pay me $50 a week every time. Pretty soon, another neighbor asked me to take care of his beagle when he went on vacation, and then *another* neighbor asked me. Some people needed help getting enough exercise for their dogs, so I started walking one dog every day after school, and I earned $20 a week to do it. In just a couple months, I earned more than $200 from my dog business!

I started thinking: What should I spend my money on? There's a pair of jeans I've been wanting, so at first I thought I would get them. And then I thought I'd probably get some more clothes to go with them. And then maybe I'd take my four besties out to see a movie, and then . . .

And then one night I saw a documentary that changed the way I looked at things. It was all about how many dogs are put to sleep every year because they don't have homes. It made me so sad I cried while watching it. I asked Mom what I could do to help those dogs, and she said I should visit the local animal shelter and ask them. So that's what I did—and that's when I realized that I could donate money to help the Humane Society give more dogs a home.

I decided I would rather help those dogs than buy new jeans. So I told my mom I was going to give *all* my money to the animal shelter. But Mom said I had to save some money to help pay for the overnight trip I want to take with the school band. And she told me I might want to keep a little money for everyday expenses and fun—like going to the movies with friends. She told me about the Three Thirds plan, and I thought, *That sounds like the plan for me.*

Today, I save one-third of my earnings for my band trip. I spend about one-third having fun with my friends. And every month, I send one-third of my income to the animal shelter. The shelter was so grateful they even put my picture on their Wall of Fame!

Your own plan doesn't have to be exactly like the 30-30-30-10 plan or the Three Thirds plan. Those are good plans to follow as models, but you can tweak either one. Maybe you do the Three Thirds plan, but you're saving for something that you're really excited about, like a new bike. So you put a little extra into savings for a few months. Or maybe you choose the 30-30-30-10 plan, but you put 30 percent toward donations and only 10 percent toward spending. Or your portions are 30-30-20-20.

Whatever you do, your plan should help you meet your goals—whether you're saving for a big purchase or helping out a cause you feel strongly about.

Keeping Track

Not every budget plan is the same—but there *is* one way that they are all alike. All budgets require you to stick to your plan. That's why they call a budget a *plan*, instead of, say, an *idea*. A budget isn't just a great idea that you keep in your head. It's a plan that you need to stay on top of and keep track of.

So how exactly should you keep track of your budget?
There are many ways to do this.

The Envelope Method

This is one of the simplest ways to keep track of your money.
Here's what you'll need: three or four envelopes, one pen,
and . . . that's all!

If you are using the Three Thirds plan, write "Spending"
on one of the envelopes. Write "Saving" on another. And write
"Donating" on the third. Then every time you get money,
stick one-third of it into each envelope.

Using the 30-30-30-10 plan? Then you use four envelopes,
labeled "Spending," "Saving for Short-Term Goals," "Saving
for Long-Term Goals," and "Donating," and divide your
money according to your budget plan.*

However, the envelope method works best if you're on
the Three Thirds plan. You just have one envelope for all your
saved money. It doesn't really matter if you know exactly what
you're saving for. The important thing is, you're keeping your
saving and donating funds separate from your spending fund.
That way you won't accidentally spend too much.

* *

*Do you need to help out with your family's expenses? If so,
you can add another envelope to your stack. Label it "Family
Expenses." When you get money, put some of it in that envelope.

The Chart Method

This method is a little more complicated than the envelope
method. You can use it if your budget is, well, a little more
complicated. Here are some examples of why that might be
the case for you:

- **You earn money from several sources.** Maybe you get an allowance each week, you have a regular babysitting job one afternoon a week, and you often make extra babysitting money on the weekends—and you want to keep track of how much you earn from each source of income.

- **You have fixed expenses.** Fixed expenses are things you regularly spend money on. Maybe you buy your school lunch with your allowance money. Or maybe you make a monthly payment to a music streaming website.

- **You have more than one savings goal.** Maybe you're saving for a short-term goal of going to a movie with your friends in two weeks, and you're also saving for a really awesome set of headphones.

- **You like to donate to a few different charities or organizations.** Some people like to give a little money each month to several charities instead of saving up for one big donation.

If any of those examples apply to you, you might want to use a chart to keep track of your budget. Get started with one of these options:

- Grab a piece of paper and a pen or pencil and design your own chart.

- Fire up the computer. You can create a table in a word processing or spreadsheet program. Or search online for "budget templates for kids"—you'll find dozens of ready-to-fill-in budget charts. (Using a tablet? There are plenty of budget apps, too.)

- See page 66 for a blank version of the following budget chart that you can copy or print out and use.

Here's an example of how your budget chart might look:

My Budget

My Monthly Income		
Where this money came from	**How much**	**Monthly total**
Allowance	$ 7 every week	$28
Mowing my neighbor's lawn	$15 every other week	$30
Extra mowing jobs	$15 this month (one job)	$15
Total money in this month		$73
My Monthly Spending		
Music streaming service	$ 9	$ 9
Spend however I want	$17	$17
My Monthly Saving		
Short-term goal: school jacket	$14	$14
Long-term goal (I'm not sure about my long-term goal yet, but I'm saving anyway)	$14	$14
My Monthly Donating		
Global disaster relief fund	$10	$10
Local women's shelter	$ 9	$ 9
Total money out this month		$73

Whichever method you choose for tracking your budget, the important thing is to be *consistent*. Every time money comes in, put it in those envelopes or fill out your chart. If you tend to be forgetful about things like this, give yourself reminders. You can jot down a reminder in your planner or calendar. You can also set a reminder on a phone or computer. Or ask a grown-up to remind you. If you have a bank account, you could even set up a weekly trip to the bank with an adult. (See Chapter 7 for more about banking.)

CONSISTENT: not changing; done the same way every time

If you consistently track your money using a budget, you'll be less likely to stray from your plan. That way you won't "accidentally" buy a $60 video game when you only have $20 in the "Spending" part of your budget. And you'll be *more* likely to meet your goals.

Keep a Budget

You can use this chart to create your budget and stay on track. As you get or earn money, write it down in the "Where This Money Came From" section. Track the money you spend in the "My Monthly Spending" section. Write down how much money you save and donate in the other two sections. (See page 64 for an example of how to complete this chart.)

My Monthly Income		
Where this money came from	How much	Monthly total
Total money in this month		
My Monthly Spending		
My Monthly Saving		
My Monthly Donating		
Total money out this month		

Aren't You a Smartypants?
(Six Tips for Being a Smart Consumer)

5

Maybe you've heard that nobody likes a smartypants. That *may* be true if you're talking about people who always need to prove that they know everything and generally act like know-it-alls.

But there's another kind of smartypants, and it's definitely a good kind to be. It's a smartypants spender—someone who doesn't waste his or her money, but uses it wisely to achieve goals. And guess what? A smartypants spender is not some rare, exotic species that lives only on faraway desert islands. It is a happy, satisfied person. And it's someone you can become.

CONSUMER: someone who buys goods and services

This chapter will give you a few simple guidelines to help you think like a smartypants and be a wise *consumer*. But first, take this quick quiz to see how much (or how little) of a smart shopper you already are. Write your answers on a separate sheet of paper.

$ Smartypants Spender Quiz

1. It's Saturday, and you just got your weekly $10 allowance. You're feeling pretty rich. You're also feeling kind of hungry. Your best friend suggests going to the corner store for some snacks — only he doesn't have any money. Do you say:

   A. "Sounds great! I've got $10, so I can treat."

   B. "I can't blow all of my money for the week in one day. Let's see what kind of snacks I have at my house."

2. You just got $50 for your birthday from your grandma! Now you can finally buy that sweet catcher's mitt you've been wanting. You already did your research and you know that it costs $40. So you'll even have a little money left over. Your mom takes you to the sporting goods store. But when you get there, you see that the price has gone up. Now the glove costs $48. Do you:

   A. Shrug, say, "Whatever," and spend all your cash.

   B. Ask your mom to help you research the price at other stores — even though that means you may have to wait another day or two to get your glove.

3. You've been saving up your money for weeks for a video game you've had your eye on. You know exactly how much it costs, and when you arrive at the store you find it. But then you notice there's a "Collector's Edition" on the shelf right next to it. It's $10 more, but it looks like it comes with free character figures. They look really cool. Do you:

   A. Grab the Collector's Edition and head for the checkout, spending $10 more than you had planned.

B. Take a minute to read the fine print on the Collector's Edition and notice that it doesn't actually come with those characters. It just offers you a chance to order them for another $20.

Quiz Answers

Okay, maybe you've figured this out already (in which case, you're at least partly a smartypants shopper): The smartypants answer to every question is B.

If you answered B to every question, you're either a hotshot smartypants spender or a seriously smart quiz taker. (Both are good skills to have!) But if you're like most kids, you answered A to one or two of the questions—or you at least thought about it. Take a look at this table to learn a little more about the spending traps those A answers describe.

Watch Out—It's a Spending Trap!

Quiz question	If you answered ...	Then you might be ...
1. What do you do when your friend suggests spending your allowance on snacks?	A. "Sounds great! I've got $10, so I can treat."	... a **too-generous** spender. That means you often spend money on others in order to have fun.
2. What do you do when you see the catcher's mitt you want for $8 more than you thought it was?	A. Shrug, say, "Whatever," and spend all your birthday cash.	... an **impatient** spender. That means you don't take the time to find the best deal.
3. What do you do when you notice a more expensive Collector's Edition of a game you planned to buy?	A. Grab the Collector's Edition and head for the checkout, spending $10 more than you had planned.	... an **impulsive** spender. That means you sometimes buy without thinking it through.

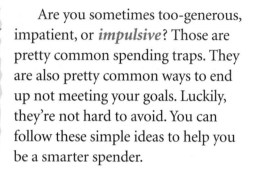

IMPULSIVE: doing something based on a sudden urge and without thinking about it

Are you sometimes too-generous, impatient, or *impulsive*? Those are pretty common spending traps. They are also pretty common ways to end up not meeting your goals. Luckily, they're not hard to avoid. You can follow these simple ideas to help you be a smarter spender.

Tips for Avoiding Spending Traps

If you're . . .	Then you might . . .	But instead, you can . . .
a **too-generous** spender	. . . often want to buy gifts or other items for your friends and family. After all, you like them and you want them to like you, too. And spending money together is fun. What's a little money when it comes to friendship?	. . . find other ways to let people know you value them. Invite them to do things that don't cost money. True friends won't feel good if you wreck your budget for them, anyway. They'd feel better if you were generous with your time and friendship . . . and fair with your money.
an **impatient** spender	. . . usually go to the closest store or most popular website to buy things, without checking around for a better deal.	. . . do more research before making purchases. Look up prices at more than one store or website. Think about which features you really need.
an **impulsive** spender	. . . often purchase things that you hadn't planned on buying. (And you might realize later that you didn't really need or want them.)	. . . make plans in advance for how you're going to spend your money. When you see something you want, tell yourself, *I'll think about it for one day. If I still want it tomorrow, I'll check around to get the best deal.*

Once you know what kind of spending traps you tend to fall into, it's easier to start making wiser choices. Read on to see more tips for spending smarts.

Tip 1: Be Thoughtful About What You Buy

Think about what you're going to buy before you go to a store or other place—like a movie theater or a park with a snack bar. Think, too, before you order something online. When you plan your spending in advance, you'll almost always end up being happier with your purchases.

Being thoughtful also means researching your purchases—big and small. For big purchases, like high-tech speakers or trendy boots, it's smart to read reviews online. Check prices at different stores, and think carefully about whether you really need the item. For smaller purchases like phone cases, purses, bracelets, or action figures, you still need to do some research. Always double-check advertisements and packaging. Make sure you know exactly what you're getting. Often, toys are packaged in huge boxes, but the toys themselves turn out not to be as big as they seem. Or the toy doesn't have as many pieces as you think it will. Just because something is pictured on the packaging doesn't mean it's included with the purchase.

List the Pros and Cons

If you're thinking about making a big purchase, or even a smaller one, write a list of pros and cons. On one side of your list are the pros. These are reasons to make the purchase. On the other side are the cons—reasons *not* to. Doing this can give you a clearer picture of what the purchase would mean to you.

Tip 2: Don't Give In to Peer Pressure

Does it ever seem like everyone else has tons of fashionable things that you don't have? It can be hard when you feel like you can't afford the clothes, video games, and devices that others can. It can be even worse if your friends pressure you to buy certain items—or act like you're not cool if you don't have them.

Maybe a bunch of your friends have the same video game and play together online. They talk about it all the time. They share all sorts of inside jokes about the game and act like you're missing out. But if you don't like that game, or if you don't

PEER PRESSURE: influence from your friends urging you to think or act a certain way

want to spend the money on it (or can't afford to), you can feel good about saying no. Doing so is being true to yourself. When you're true to yourself, you don't buy something just to fit in. And you don't change the way you act just to make other people like you. You act like *you*.

Of course, resisting *peer pressure* isn't easy. If it seems like everybody is doing the same thing or has the same product, you might feel left out. It might even be true that you *are* being left out of that particular thing. But it can help to remember that trends tend to change quickly. People get tired of the video game. Those fancy earbuds or headbands begin to seem less important. Or people get tired of eating super-hot bacon-flavored cheese curls. If you stay true to yourself, you will be the same good person you are now when the trend dies out.

It also helps to think about your reasons for not buying a certain item. Maybe you don't think having more things makes a person cool. Maybe you really don't care about those things. Or maybe you have more important ways to spend your money. Think about your reasons ahead of time. And the next time someone makes a comment about you not having that oh-so-important item, you'll know what to say— "I'm just not into that," or "I've got something else I'm saving for." You might be surprised to find out how much others respect your opinions when you dare to be different.

Tip 3: Understand Advertising

One way companies get kids to buy their clothes, toys, cereal, candy, or other items is by showing them commercials that make the products seem really popular, fun, or delicious.

Think about this: The average American kid sees between 25,000 and 40,000 commercials per year. If each commercial is 30 seconds long, that means you could be watching ads for about 20,000 minutes, or 333 hours each year! If you spent that time doing homework, you'd . . . well, you might not have much time to watch commercials. (But you'd have great grades.)

Some commercials show kids having the best time. Maybe they're playing with some super-cool toy like a high-powered water blaster. Or they're grinning from ear to ear while eating a delicious-looking (but terrible-for-you) fast food burger. Another favorite commercial trick is to make it seem like you'll be extra popular if you buy a certain item—like a name-brand hoodie, a video game, or even a type of gum.

Check out the commercial for a made-up product on the next page. Does it sound familiar?

You know it's a commercial. You know they're trying to sell you something. And you're no dummy. So what's the big deal?

Here's What's Really Going On

People who make commercials are no dummies, either. So why are they spending about $17 billion a year advertising to kids in the United States? Because it works.

Commercial makers have lots of tricks to make you want their products. Three of the big ones are shown in the commercial for Super Awesome Sneakers.

1. **They only show the good times.** You never see a kid in a commercial who is struggling with the instructions or

accidentally snapping off a breakable part. The girl in the Super Awesome Sneakers commercial is smiling like she's having a great time. Maybe Super Awesome Sneakers will give you a blister on your big toe. Or maybe those shoes wear out very quickly. But you won't see any of that in the commercial.

2. **They exaggerate the benefits.** Notice how the girl in the Super Awesome Sneakers commercial is running faster than anyone, even the dog? See how she leaps a huge bush? There's even a superhero sound effect to enhance her leap. *Whoosh!* The commercial doesn't actually say that the shoes will make you run faster or jump higher. But it sure does hint at it.

3. **They suggest you'll be popular.** Businesses know that kids want to be liked by their peers. That's why many commercials show groups of kids surrounding the kid who has the product. Maybe they're trying to see it, or they're telling the kid how great it is. In the commercial for Super Awesome Sneakers, the other kids all want to run with the girl.

All these tricks work. And all the money companies spend on advertising is worth it to them. Research shows that children in the United States spend around $18 billion dollars a year. Teens spend about $160 billion a year. Are you keeping track of all this money? Well hold on, there's more. Kids and teens also influence up to $670 billion a year in their families' spending. (That means their family spends the money, but the kids have a say in what they spend it on.) That's $848 billion dollars that are spent by or for young people in the United States alone. And you thought the $17 billion spent on advertising was a lot.

What Can You Do About It?

Be aware of the ways companies make their products look and sound so great. If something seems too good to be true, it probably is. Can sneakers really make you faster and more popular? Of course not. They're just shoes.

Be Social Media Savvy

Advertising is especially clever on social media sites like Instagram and Snapchat. Companies pay big money to get information about your likes, dislikes, and past purchases. Then they send you ads for things they know you will probably like—on your Instagram page, to your phone number, or through email. Don't believe anything until you've read about it from an *unbiased* source.

UNBIASED: having a fair opinion about something without favoring one point of view

Tip 4: Give Yourself a Time-Out

No, you don't need to tell yourself to sit quietly in the corner. But making yourself wait before committing to a big purchase is a great habit to get into. This is especially true if you suddenly come up with a *brilliant* idea for something you just *have* to have.

Let's say you're at the Big Store with your mom shopping for groceries. But you stray away from the dairy aisle to the DVDs. And then you see it, bathed in a glorious light. It's a box collection of every episode of your favorite TV show. It sounds like angels are singing all around you. The box has every episode, *plus* bonus features like deleted scenes and interviews with the stars. In that moment, it feels like your life will not be complete without that boxed set. It costs $24.99— and you have the money.

Often, if you wait a day or so, your brilliant idea will seem a little less brilliant. Or that must-have item will seem a little less must-have. It helps to get a little distance from the moment. In the Big Store example, the thing to do is hold off on buying the box set that day. Help your mom finish the grocery shopping, and go home. Chances are, the next time you go to the Big Store, that DVD box set will still be there. If you still want it, you can buy it then. But you might find that the glorious light that seemed to be shining on the box the last time you were there will be a little dimmer the second time. You might just decide that it isn't worth $24.99 to you. (You've seen all the episodes, anyway.)

There's another reason to wait a little while before buying something new. Hot items like music, movies, and electronic gadgets are most expensive when they're brand-new. But they go down in price after a while. Sometimes the price goes *way* down. You might be able to order a game or buy a DVD for half the original price just by waiting a while.

Tip 5: Watch Your Online Spending

Does this sound familiar?

You and your friend are hanging out, and she shows you a game she's been playing on her phone. It looks really fun. She says if you get it, too, then you two can play against each other. So you whip out your phone and find the game in the app store. It's only $1.99, so you hit the purchase button. A few seconds later, you're playing.

Not all kids buy things online. You need a parent's permission before you do. And you need to enter a credit or debit card number. Maybe your parents help out by entering their card number. Or maybe you even have your own card for making purchases. In any case, if you do make electronic purchases, be sure to follow all of the smartypants spending tips. Buying online is just like going to a store, so research your purchases. Make spending plans in advance. Resist pressure from friends and the media. Simple enough, right?

But some kinds of online spending are very different from in-person spending. And they can be harder to keep track of and be smart about. For one thing, you might find that you spend more money than you meant to because it happens so quickly or it's so easy to do. Think about any apps, games, and music you download. Think about movies you buy or rent to stream. These purchases are often made with a simple keystroke. *Click,* you're done—and the money is gone.

Then there are those purchases you make while playing a game or using an app you already own. It might cost a few cents to get a new ability in your online battle game. Or it's a dollar or two to get some extra cat toys in your pet-collecting app game. But these little purchases can add up quickly.

Other times, when you buy physical objects online, you may forget to add up the shipping costs. Or you might be tempted to spend more on things you don't really need or want, just to get free shipping.

It can also be risky to have money all loaded up in an online store just waiting to be spent. Maybe your uncle got you a gift card for your birthday, or an adult put money into a gaming account for you. The money is there, it's easy to spend, and it hardly seems real. Sometimes it doesn't even feel like you're spending money at all when you buy things online.

It may not feel like it—but you are! At some point, you'll run out of your loaded-up balance. Or you'll end up in hot water with your parents when they get a bill for $40 worth of online cat toys they did *not* order. So it pays to shop online like a smartypants. You'll thank yourself next time you see something that you *really* want or need and you have enough money to buy it.

Tip 6: Beware the Sneak-Attack Snack Attack

We all need to eat. And you can buy food almost everywhere, from your neighborhood store to vending machines, the movies, the mall, the park, the pool. . .

Come to think of it, there aren't too many places where you *can't* buy a snack.

If you're like most kids, you probably spend a good chunk of your change on snacks. They're yummy and easy to get. It's hard to resist! All you have to do is slip a couple dollars into the vending machine. Before you know it, you're unwrapping those chocolate mini-donuts. Delicious! Why not put a couple more bucks in the slot for a sports drink? Actually, those onion chips look great, too.

Next thing you know, you've fed six dollars into that vending machine. And all you have to show for it is a belly full of empty calories and a ruined dinner. Classic junk food blunder.

Guarding Against Sneak–Attack Snack Attacks

Tricky spot	Sneak-Attack Snack Attack risk
Walking home from school 	Your group of friends stops at a convenience store on the way home every day. You're always starving. You usually just buy a bag of chips ($1.19) and a soda ($1.79). No big deal, right? Except that adds up to about $15 a week— or a whopping $60 dollars a month.
At the movies 	Mmm, nothing goes with a movie like popcorn. And candy. And of course a drink to wash it all down. But when the popcorn costs $7.50, the candy costs $4.00, and a medium soda is $4.50, you've easily spent more on snacks than on your movie ticket.
At the vending machine	After gymnastics practice, your favorite thing to do is get a sports drink and snack from the vending machine. Hey, you just spent a LOT of energy— you deserve it!

What you could do instead

Sure, you're hungry after school—but a little planning can go a long way. Drop a healthier snack in your backpack before you leave for school in the morning. That way you can avoid the junk food—and junk spending. Try a cheese stick, granola bar, or even a container of pretzels from home.

Sound like too much work? You could try skipping the snack—or cutting down. Take baby steps and cut out the soda one week, then the chips the next week. Then on Fridays, go ahead and treat yourself. You'll still save nearly $50 a month.

You have a couple options here. You could skip the snack. Eat something before you leave home and remind yourself you're not hungry when you get to the theater. (Need help? Think about what else you can do with all the money you're saving.)

You can also save a lot of money by cutting back a little. Go for the popcorn OR the candy. Ask for a cup for water instead of a soda. Better yet, split a medium or large popcorn with your friend. Chances are you'll both have plenty, and it will save you both money.

Actually, health experts say you're better off drinking plain water after a workout. And that's free.

If you really don't want to give up your sports drink, buy some powdered mix for home. You can probably get a whole canister for about the price of one bottle at the vending machine. Before practice, mix it up in your water bottle. Add some ice, and you're good to go.

Buying snacks is fun and tasty. But it's one of the worst ways to spend your money. For one thing, your family probably keeps healthier food around the kitchen. If so, you can snack at home to save money, plus get some health benefits.

Even when you have to buy your own snacks, you can usually save a lot by avoiding convenience snacks. Take a look at the table on the previous pages for three tricky snack spots. It gives tips for keeping your money safe from Sneak-Attack Snack Attacks.

If it's starting to sound like the message of this chapter is to never spend your money, it's not. The message is to be *deliberate* about spending your money. That means thinking about your purchases before you make them. It means having a realistic idea of what you're getting (and *not* getting) and finding the best price. And it means understanding whether buying an item would mean being true to yourself.

DELIBERATE: thoughtful, careful, and planned

But that is not to say you should never spend your money, even on something slightly silly, like cat toys for your pet app or fancy sneakers. If you've been smart with your money, it's nice to reward yourself with a treat now and then. If buying the cat toys will make your game a lot more fun and it fits into your budget, go for it. As for those new shoes, maybe they will look great on you. Maybe they'll feel good, too. (Just don't expect to leap bushes like a super hero.)

My Money Went Where?

(Being a Mindful Consumer)

Being smart about your money is important. Smartypants spenders can usually figure out how to reach their goals *and* have some fun with their money. They can manage it all without too much trouble. If your goals are important to you, that's a pretty big deal.

But here's another big deal when it comes to spending money: being mindful. What the heck does that mean? It means using your *mind* to think about all the things that happen as a result of your spending. It means thinking not only about how spending the money affects you, but also about how it affects others—and the world. Your choices make a difference.

If you're still not sure what being mindful means, that's okay. Read this Choose Your Own Spending Ending story and see if it gives you some ideas.

Choose Your Own Spending Ending

Family Fun Day

It's a beautiful summer Saturday, and your family decides to do something fun together.

Your mom suggests going to the zoo. She loves seeing the big cats, and the howler monkeys always crack everyone up. Plus, you can get slushies at the snack bar—a family favorite. You love the zoo, too. But after seeing the polar bear exhibit you always feel kind of sad. Those two huge bears are cooped up in a small environment. They just swim back and forth in the little pool all day as if they wish they could go farther. They look bored and unhappy. Still, the rest of the zoo is fun.

Your little sister wants to go to the pool. It's a hot day, so cooling down in the water would be nice. They have a decent snack bar there, but it's not as good as the zoo's snack bar. They don't have slushies.

Your mom says you can cast the deciding vote.

What do you do?

1 >   You've already been to the pool a couple times this summer, so the zoo would be more of a treat. Plus, you love to see your mom cracking up at the howler monkeys. You figure you can just skip the polar bears so you don't

get sad about them. "Let's go to the zoo!" you say. ***Turn to
Ending 1*** *on page 93.*

2 You don't feel right about those polar bears, but you're
not sure if it really is a problem. Maybe they're perfectly
happy. So you do a quick search online and find an article
that explains how a lot of people—including wildlife
experts—agree with you. Many zoos are very humane and
do a great job taking care of animals. But those polar bears
are a problem. It is not *ethical* to coop them up in such a
small space. You decide
you don't want to spend
money at a place that treats
animals that way. "Grab the
sunscreen," you say. "Let's
go to the pool." ***Turn to
Ending 2*** *on page 94.*

> **ETHICAL:**
> trying to do
> the right thing;
> morally right
> or good

Your Part in the Cycle

Whenever you buy something, you become part of a cycle.
Here's how it goes:

1. Something gets made.

2. Then it gets bought.

3. Then it gets used.

4. Then it either gets thrown away, reused, resold,
   or recycled.

That cycle can be great. Hey, it's how people make money.
But it can also be not so great. Sometimes making things
causes harm to the earth and the environment. Other times,
companies that make things don't treat their workers well.

Or they don't treat animals well. Sometimes, the *making* of an item might be perfectly fine. But the item itself can cause harm. (Think tobacco, sugar, or plastic that doesn't get recycled.)

Take a look at these examples of spending *consequences*:

- You bought a 32-ounce soda pop. Hey, it was only 10 cents more than the 16-ouncer! But now you feel like you might throw up. *Guess what? You're experiencing a health consequence.*

- You bought a new pair of jeans. But then you found out that they were made in another country by 10-year-olds who each earned less than a dollar a month for their work. *Even though you didn't know it at the time, your money supported illegal child labor.*

- You ordered a chicken sandwich at a fast-food chain. It turns out that the food chain buys its chicken from producers who keep the chickens in overcrowded cages. *Your sandwich might have tasted fine, but your cash supported the unhealthy and unethical treatment of animals.*

- You bought a new pair of headphones. After ripping off the plastic wrapping, taking the headphones out of the cardboard box, and removing the foam protective wrap, your recycling bin is practically full. *If you had bought a used pair of headphones, there probably would have been no packaging—and you would have helped protect the environment.*

CONSEQUENCE:
the result of an action

Yes, You Can Do Something!

Ready to make a positive impact with your spending? You can do a lot to reduce the negative consequences of your spending. Three main ways are by buying less, buying from responsible companies when you can, and buying products that do as little harm as possible.

Buy Less

Making a difference with your spending doesn't have to be a huge, life-changing act. It's not hard to simply buy less of something. Every time you *don't* buy something, you're saving the earth just a little bit. You're helping cut down on the number of things that get made, used, and thrown away.

Here's an example. Let's say you love colored rubber wristbands. You've already got about 20. But now there are new colors, and those new colors would look pretty great on your wrist.

But if you're trying to be mindful about your spending, you might think about all the wristbands that are floating around in the world already. You might think about what's going to happen when you get tired of wearing them. Will you throw them out? Will you be able to find a way to recycle them? Maybe you could come up with a way to start recycling some right now.

Instead of buying a dozen new colors, you decide to twist together a few that you already own. That makes a cool new style. Even better, you're saving the world from a little more garbage down the road.

And no, wristbands are not the world's worst products. But every little thing we buy adds up. Even food packaging produces waste. For any item you're thinking about buying, ask yourself: *Do I really need it? Could I get by with less of it? Could I buy it less often?*

If you cut back your purchasing just a little bit, you are making a difference. Nice job!

Buy Used Products

A different way to buy less is to buy used. When you buy something that has already been used, you help keep it from getting thrown away—and ending up in a *landfill*.

Does "used" sound bad to you? Don't worry! Lots of used items can be just as good as new ones. Used games, books, and even clothing can all feel "new" to you. You can find great used products at garage sales, yard sales, and stores that specialize in selling second-hand items.

LANDFILL: an area where waste is buried in the ground, potentially poisoning the land and water, or releasing greenhouse gasses that affect climate change

Buy from Responsible Companies

What are "responsible companies"? They are companies that try hard not to harm people, animals, or the earth. These companies are ethical—they care about doing the right thing.

To learn whether a company is responsible, you could type "is [company name] ethical" into an Internet search engine and get some answers. Apps, books, and websites can also help you. For example, the Good Shopping Guide website, at thegoodshoppingguide.com, compares hundreds of companies on issues such as their environmental, animal welfare, and human rights records.

Then, you can think about the issues you care about and the companies you've researched whenever you're thinking about buying something. This will make you a more informed consumer. That will help the earth—and the people and animals that live there.

What issues should you think about when researching companies and deciding where to spend your money? The following list covers some of the biggest issues and questions. (See pages 101–102 for a version of this list you can print out or photocopy. Use it to record answers when you research a company.)

Responsible Companies, Responsible Choices

Companies must make decisions about many of these issues. You may not want to give your money to a company that makes decisions you disagree with.

Human rights: Does the company use child labor? Do employees work in unhealthy or dangerous conditions? Do employees earn fair wages and benefits?

The environment: Does the company practice *sustainability*? Is it careful about the pollution it creates? Does the company try to reduce its impact on global climate change? Does it farm in a way that's good for the environment? Does it use renewable energy? Or does it dump toxic waste or destroy forests?

SUSTAINABILITY: the act of producing goods in a way that does as little harm to the environment and to communities as possible

Animal welfare: Does the company treat animals humanely (in a caring way, and without hurting them)? Or does it use animal testing? Do the company's operations hurt animal habitats?

Community involvement: Does the company donate some of its profits to organizations that help others or the environment? Are its employees encouraged to volunteer or give back to the community in any way?

Political support: Which candidates do the company's owners and leaders give money to? Does the company try to influence lawmakers to change laws (or to prevent laws from changing)? Which laws? And why?

Social justice: Does the company have a history of discrimination or harassment? Has it been in trouble with the law? These are signs that a company is unethical.

For the most part, the spending decisions you make affect you and those who are close to you. You will probably feel better if you don't give your money to a company that destroys rainforests to make its products. You might also raise awareness of an issue by talking about it with your friends, family, and teachers. Maybe your friends join you in *boycotting* that company.

Sometimes our actions add up and go beyond our town or our circle of friends. If enough kids boycott that rainforest-destroying company, the company will notice that it's selling fewer products. If enough people talk about the boycott on blogs or social media, the company will eventually find out about that, too. Sometimes someone

BOYCOTT: to refuse to buy or use something as a way to protest how a company does business

well-known, like a celebrity or a newspaper writer, will talk about the problem. The company will *definitely* notice then. And if they want to keep selling their products, they will make a change.

You don't have to spread the word so widely unless you feel very strongly about an issue. Then you can speak out and raise awareness. But the way most of us make a difference from day to day is with our money.

Remember when you were deciding how to spend your summer day? Check out your spending endings below.

See Your Spending Ending

Family Fun Day

Ending 1

You have a great time at the zoo. When you get to the howler monkeys, your mom laughs so hard she cries a little bit. You have a blue-and-red swirled slushie for a treat. You do stop by the polar bear exhibit, and it is just as sad as you remember.

When you get home that night, you feel unhappy about the day even though most of it was fun. You do some research online and learn that many people are boycotting the zoo until the animals are treated better—especially the polar bears. An activist is quoted as saying, "When we spend money at that zoo, we are reinforcing what they've always done. But if enough of us decide to spend our entertainment dollars elsewhere, we force them to change their ways." You think about all the money your family spent at the zoo that day, and you feel bad. You decide to talk to your mom about avoiding the zoo, or maybe even working to help the polar bears.

The End

Ending 2

You have a blast at the pool, but while you and your sister swim back and forth underwater, you think about those polar bears at the zoo. When you get home, you add your name to a petition online. It is trying to get the zoo to move the bears to a different zoo or expand their environment. At school the next week, you tell a friend what you learned. Your friend tells another friend. You even end up talking about it in language arts class. Other kids get excited about signing the petition. You feel proud for being mindful about your spending. And you feel like you're helping make a positive change.

The End

Buy Products That Don't Do Harm

When you choose to buy products that do as little harm as possible, your choices aren't necessarily about the companies that make the products. Instead, they're about the products themselves. Think about drinks that come in plastic bottles, which are terrible for the earth. Try to buy things in bulk when possible. This cuts down on packaging. Try to avoid foods that are packaged for individual use, like personal pudding cups and juice boxes. These use the most packaging of all. And even if some of it's recyclable, a whole lot of that packaging gets tossed in the garbage and ends up in a dump. Many nonfood products, like toys and electronics, also come in wasteful packaging.

Here are some more tips for buying products that don't do harm. Whenever possible, follow these guidelines:

- Avoid products that are tested on animals.
- Look for products made with organic ingredients (natural and not made with chemicals that harm people or the environment).

- Choose products that are in containers made from recycled paper or plastic and/or that can be recycled. Buy products that have minimal packaging.

Go Local with Food!

One way to be a mindful spender is to try buying locally produced or locally grown food when you can. This food doesn't have to travel as far to get from the farm or the factory to the store. That means it takes less fuel to ship it, which is better for the environment. Buying locally produced food also helps provide jobs for people in your own community. It's usually fresher, too. However, locally produced food can sometimes be more expensive. So check your budget to make sure that going local works for you.

How to Be Mindful

As you can see, you can consider many details and concerns when you work on being a mindful shopper. But don't let that overwhelm you. In many ways, being a mindful consumer boils down to two simple guidelines:

- **Positive purchasing.** This means buying from companies that make their products in a way that is good for the environment, for human rights, and for the consumers who use them.

- **Negative purchasing.** This means avoiding products and companies that you know go against your values.

Don't worry about being perfect when it comes to mindful shopping. Every purchasing decision makes a difference, but you can't fix the world on your own. Decide to be as mindful as you can, within reason. You'll still be making a positive contribution.

Making Mindful Donations

It's also important to be mindful when you make donations. That means carefully choosing which organizations get the privilege of receiving your money.

When deciding where to donate, start by choosing one of the following categories: organizations that help people, animals, or the environment. Is one of these areas more important to you than the others?

- **People:** Organizations that help people include those that do research to cure or prevent diseases like cancer, or that provide food for people who need it. Others provide education, help people in emergencies, and more.

- **Animals:** These organizations help find homes for pets and provide shelter to animals that need it. They may provide medical attention and protect animals from abuse and neglect. Some speak out against the cruel testing of products on animals.

- **Environment:** These organizations may work to protect rainforests or work to create laws to reduce harmful pollution. Many plant trees, work to reduce water and air pollution, and support other environmental causes.

In all three categories, you can choose a charity that is local, national, or international. An example of a charity that is local to your area is a clothing donation center or water protection organization. On the other hand, many disaster relief charities are international. Your money is more likely to make an immediate impact if you keep it local. But sometimes larger organizations are the only ones that support the cause you are interested in.

You can also make a more visible difference by choosing an organization with specific goals. In other words, it might be easy to donate to a big, general environmental charity. But you might feel more satisfied if you give your money to an organization that is working to clean up a lake in your community.

Once you know what kind of organization you want to donate to, do some research on charities that fit into that category. Say you want to donate to an environmental organization, and you want to keep it local. You have learned about some problems with air pollution in your area, and you'd like to help fix that. You can research online to identify organizations that are working on that issue.

Now, keep digging until you learn more about those organizations. One place to look is the Charity Navigator website at charitynavigator.org. This website gives lots of advice for choosing charities. It looks at how effective and ethical they are. And it provides a list of questions to ask before making a donation to a charity.

REAL-WORLD KID

Freddi Zeiler

When Freddi Zeiler was 12 years old, her family moved to Topanga Canyon, a town in the mountains of California. Freddi loved the beauty of the area, and she enjoyed hiking in the state parks nearby. She saw beautiful trees, streams, and wildlife. But she also saw litter all over. She decided to make a difference by taking trash bags along on her hikes and picking up the trash.

Soon, Freddi realized she wanted to do more. She began donating half her allowance to environmental charities. But because her allowance wasn't very much money, she wanted to make sure she donated her money to the right charity. So she started researching charities online. She also called charities on the phone to ask them questions. One question she asked was, "How much of each donated dollar goes directly to the cause?"

When Freddi was done, she had a *lot* of information about a lot of charities—enough information to fill a book. So that's what she did! Freddi wrote *A Kid's Guide to Giving,* which covers three main topics: Why to give, how to choose a charity, and how to contribute. The book outlines more than 100 charities for kids to consider.

One question to ask is what percentage of donations goes to *overhead*. Some charities have a lot of overhead—money they spend running the organization as opposed to putting it directly toward the cause. That overhead money might pay for employee salaries, the charity's offices, or fundraising.

It's up to donors—that's you!—to decide for themselves how much overhead is reasonable. But a good rule of thumb is that a charity should spend less than 30 percent of donations on overhead. That means at least 70 percent should go toward the actual cause. So if you donate $10 to a cancer prevention charity, that organization should be putting at least $7 toward cancer research and less than $3 toward running the organization.

OVERHEAD:
money that a business or organization spends on things that keep it running, such as salaries or rent

Is a Company Responsible?

Use these questions to help you research whether a company is responsible. Type the company's name and one of the questions below into an Internet search engine, and check NO or YES depending on what you learn. Or visit your local library and search for information there. Some issues might be harder than others to research. If you run into challenges, you can ask an adult to help you. If you still can't find reliable information on a certain issue, check the ? box. In other cases, some questions may not apply to the company you are researching. You can just skip those questions. Add any other information about the company that is important to you in the Notes section at the end.

Company Name: _____

Human Rights

Does the company use child labor? ☐ NO ☐ YES ☐ ?

Do employees work in unhealthy or dangerous conditions? ☐ NO ☐ YES ☐ ?

Do employees earn fair wages and benefits? ☐ NO ☐ YES ☐ ?

The Environment

Does the company practice sustainability? ☐ NO ☐ YES ☐ ?

Does the company work to limit the pollution it creates? ☐ NO ☐ YES ☐ ?

Does the company try to reduce its impact on global climate change? ☐ NO ☐ YES ☐ ?

Does the company farm in a way that's good for the environment? ☐ NO ☐ YES ☐ ?

Does the company use renewable or sustainable energy sources? ☐ NO ☐ YES ☐ ?

Does the company dump toxic waste or destroy rainforests or other natural areas? ☐ NO ☐ YES ☐ ?

Animal Welfare

Does the company treat animals humanely (in a caring way and without hurting them) ☐ NO ☐ YES ☐ ?

→

Is a Company Responsible? (continued)

Does the company use animal testing? ☐ NO ☐ YES ☐ ?

Do the company's operations hurt
    animal habitats? ☐ NO ☐ YES ☐ ?

Community Involvement

Does the company donate some of its
    profits to organizations that help
    others or the environment? ☐ NO ☐ YES ☐ ?

Are the company's employees encouraged
    to volunteer or give back to the
    community in any way? ☐ NO ☐ YES ☐ ?

Social Justice

Does the company have a history of
    discrimination or harassment? ☐ NO ☐ YES ☐ ?

Has the company been in trouble with the law? ☐ NO ☐ YES ☐ ?

Political Support

Which political candidates do the company's owners and leaders
support? _____

_____

_____

Does the company try to influence lawmakers to change laws (or to
prevent laws from changing)? ☐ NO ☐ YES

Which laws? And why? _____

_____

_____

NOTES: _____

_____

_____

After researching a company, review how you answered each question.
Decide whether you will feel good about buying products and services
from this company—or whether you will keep it in mind as one to avoid.

Your School for Cool Money Tools
(Banking and Borrowing)

Bzzzzzzzzzzzzzzz!

There's the bell! Come on in, students, and have a seat. Welcome to the School for Cool Money Tools. Instead of saws and hammers, these tools are things like bank accounts and spending cards. You can't use them to build a tree house, but you *can* use them to build up your money smarts. They can help you track your money, save it more effectively, and spend it wisely.

So go ahead and open your textbook to page, uh, well, *this* page. Who would like to read aloud? You in the back. Thank you. Please start with the first Cool Tool.

Cool Tool: Savings Accounts

When you put your money into a savings account, you are asking a bank to hold onto it for you. That helps you save. But to understand how bank accounts work, you first need to know how banks work.

What's a Bank?

Banks have been helping people manage their money since about 4,000 years ago. That's a pretty long history! Of course, back then a bank was a person who loaned crops to a farmer until his own crops came in. Today, banks offer a lot of different services to people and businesses. They loan money, accept deposits, pay interest, exchange the money of one country for the money of another . . . and plenty more.

The main thing a bank does, though, is borrow and lend money. When people—or businesses—borrow from a bank, they pay the bank *interest*. Interest is a fee you pay for borrowing money. It's usually a percentage of the amount borrowed. That's how banks make their money: They earn interest.

INTEREST:
the charge on borrowed money

But interest also works the other way. People who deposit money into a bank *earn* interest. When you deposit money into a bank account, you're lending your money to the bank. So the bank pays you interest on that money. The more money you deposit—or the longer you agree to leave it in the bank—the more interest you can earn.

A Tool to Help You Save

Banks offer many different kinds of accounts. At most banks, kids can open joint accounts with a parent, guardian, or other adult. The best kind of account for kids is usually a savings account. That's where you put your money into the bank and earn interest on it. A savings account may be a good tool to help you manage your money for several reasons. With a savings account, you can usually:

- Open and use it for free
- Open it with just a little bit of money
- Pay little or nothing in fees
- Deposit (add) money as often as you like
- Earn interest
- Make several free withdrawals (taking money out of your account) each month*

*But remember, you're trying to *save* money. Don't use this perk too often.

When you open an account, you'll get a little book called a register or savings passbook to help you keep track of your money. Every time you deposit or withdraw money, write it down in your register. This helps you keep track of your *balance*. If you make deposits often, a register lets you see how fast your money is growing. And if you make withdrawals too often, it can let you know when you're about to run out of money!

You can also track your bank account online. The adult you opened your account with can help you get a *password* to view your account on the bank's website. Then you can

BALANCE: the amount of money in an account

PASSWORD: a word, set of numbers, or combination of letters and numbers that you keep secret and use to access something private, such as a bank account check your account balance at any time from any computer, smartphone, or tablet. You can compare your balance to what you have written down in your register or passbook. This can help you know whether you are doing a good job of tracking all your deposits and withdrawals. Then you know if you're meeting your budget goals—or if you need to change your money habits.

Cool Tool: Checking Accounts

A checking account is another kind of bank account. It lets you spend the money you have deposited in the bank much more easily than a savings account does. With a checking account, you can spend your money by writing *checks* or using a debit card. When you write a check or swipe a debit card, money is electronically subtracted from your account. You may have to pay a small fee to keep your money in a checking account.

CHECK: a written note that tells your bank to pay money from your account. When you have a checking account, the bank gives you checks with your account number on them. You fill out the checks with information about specific payments.

You are more likely to use a *debit card* than checks. A debit card is a plastic card with a magnetic strip on the back. You can swipe the strip in a card reader at a store. When you do that, the amount of your purchase is automatically taken out of

DEBIT CARD: a plastic card that is issued by a bank and that you can use to buy things. The money you spend is taken out of your bank account at the time of the purchase.

your account. To use the card for an online purchase, you type in the account number from the front of the card.

Debit cards can be used at almost any store, restaurant, or other business. When you use a debit card, money is transferred electronically from your account to the account of the business you're paying.

Note: Call your bank to find out how old you have to be to open a checking account or use a debit card. At some banks, you have to be 14.

Easy Money?

Debit cards are really convenient because you don't have to carry enough cash for your purchases. Of course, that also makes them dangerous. How so? Glad you asked . . .

 DANGER: OVERSPENDING!

It's very easy to spend money with a debit card. Let's say you're at a store and you want to buy a cereal bar. You've budgeted for buying snacks, but you don't have enough cash with you. No problem—you can use your debit card. While you're at it, you figure you might as well grab a bag of sour candy, too. You have the money in your account, so why not? You swipe your card, and . . . *beep!* The snacks are yours—and you've spent more than you meant to.

You didn't see any money change hands, so it almost feels like the snacks were free. But they weren't free, of course. That money is real, even if it's not always easy to think of it that way. If you had been paying with cash, maybe you would only have gotten the cereal bar and not overspent. Paying with cash helps most shoppers be more careful. We see those precious bills and coins leave our hands. It feels . . . final.

DANGER: FEES!

What happens if you don't have enough money in your account to cover your purchase? Usually the computer system will check to make sure you have the money to cover the charge. If you don't have enough, the transaction won't go through. That means you don't get to buy your items.

But sometimes the computer can't tell. And that's where you can get into trouble. You might still be able to buy the item, but your bank has to pay the extra money owed to the store. Then the bank will charge you a fee for doing this. Sometimes the business you're purchasing from will also charge you a fee. These fees can be between $15 and $40— each! They can add up pretty quickly to big money.

Using ATMs

Debit cards are also used at ATMs, or Automated Teller Machines. An ATM is a machine where you can withdraw money from your bank account without going to your bank. You slide in your debit card and type in your personal identification number (PIN) on a number pad. Your PIN is a secret code that you come up with. Once you enter your PIN, you can withdraw cash from your account or make a deposit. You can also check your balance.

You can only deposit into an ATM that belongs to your bank. But you can usually check your balance and withdraw

money at any ATM in the world. Be careful, though. If the ATM doesn't belong to your bank, you'll probably have to pay a fee for using it. These fees can be from $1.50 to $8.00 or even more. To avoid these fees, try to avoid ATMs that don't belong to your bank. Most ATMs have their fees printed right on them so you know what you're getting into.

Fee, Fi, Fo . . .

Wait, did you say *fee*? Fooey. You have to watch out for those.

In Chapter 2, you learned that a fee is an amount of money paid for a service. When you're the one charging the fee—such as for raking your neighbor's lawn—it's a good thing! But when you have to pay a fee, it's not so good. And banks charge all kinds of fees. Here are a few of the most common ones.

- **Overdraft fees.** If you use your debit card to spend more than you have in your account, you may be charged an overdraft fee. These fees can be up to $40. If you overdraft twice, you get charged twice. Do it again, you get charged again.

- **ATM fees.** If you use another bank's ATM to withdraw money from your account, you can be charged $1.50 to $8.00 or more. Different ATMs charge different fees.

- **Maintenance fees.** Some banks charge you every month for your checking account. These maintenance fees can be about $12.00 a month. Some banks won't charge the fee if you keep enough money in the account or meet other requirements.

- **Lost card fee.** If you lose your debit card, the bank will likely charge you to replace it.

When you use an ATM, you can ask for a printed receipt. This will show how much money you deposited or withdrew. It will also show your balance. Hold onto this receipt and remember to record the amount in your register or passbook. Doing this will help you keep track of your balance—and make sure you don't get way off track from your savings goals.

Cool Tool: Prepaid Cards

If you don't have a checking account, you can still use cards for purchases. Prepaid cards look and feel just like debit cards, and you use them the same way. Swipe the magnetic strip through a card reader at a store or type in the account number at a retail website. The difference is that the money you spend doesn't come right out of your bank account. The money has already been "loaded" onto the card by you or someone else.

Sometimes money gets loaded onto a prepaid card when you buy it. Say you're at the drugstore and you buy a $15 card to your favorite coffee shop. The $15 is loaded on the card as soon as you pay the drugstore for it. When your grandmother

gives you a gift card to the bookstore, the card was loaded with money when she paid the bookstore. Some kinds of prepaid cards can be reloaded at the store or online.

Prepaid cards are a convenient option if you don't have a bank account. They're just as easy to use as debit cards, but there are no bank fees to pay. You might have to pay fees charged by companies that sell prepaid cards, though. These can be high sometimes. And some cards can expire. So it's important to do your research.

Another benefit of a prepaid card is the fact that it isn't connected to a bank account. That means you don't have to worry about spending more than you have in your account—and being charged a fee. Once you use up the money that's been prepaid, you can't spend any more. However, there *is* a danger with a prepaid card . . .

DANGER: LOSING IT!

If you lose a prepaid card, the money on it is gone. Anyone who finds or steals the card can use it. They don't need to show any identification or prove that the card belongs to them.

Cool Tool: Credit Cards

Credit cards look like debit cards and prepaid cards. But they don't take money directly out of your bank account, and you don't have to preload them. You still get to spend money with them, though. That's because when you use a credit card to make a purchase, the credit card company pays for it up front.

Sound like a pretty sweet deal? Well, that money isn't a gift. To get a credit card, you sign an agreement to borrow money from a credit card company or bank. And you agree to repay any money you borrow. It's like getting a loan from a bank whenever you want it. But with credit cards, you have

Protect Your ID

If you order things online, it's important to be careful with your personal information. If someone gets your account information, that person can buy things with your money. Even worse is if someone gets personal information such as your social security number. That person can use the information to log into websites and pretend to be you. He or she can also open credit cards, get loans, or make purchases—all while pretending to be you.

You can protect your identity and your safety by only entering card numbers into websites with addresses that begin with https:// That "s" on the end stands for "secure," and it means the website is safe from people who might try to break into it. Use strong passwords, and don't tell them to anyone other than your parents—not even your BFF. Change your passwords often. Don't give out personal information online to anyone who asks for it—not even your name—without an adult there to help you make sure it's safe.

to pay interest on that loan if you don't pay it back within a month. And credit card interest rates can be very high.

Since you're a kid, you aren't old enough to get your own credit card. You have to be at least 18 for some cards and 21 for others. But you *can* be added to your parents' credit card accounts if they give permission. In this case, you get your own card, but it's connected to your parent's account. Your parent is responsible for any money you spend. If your parent trusts you to carry and use a card, this can be a good way for you to get experience with credit.

Another option is a store credit card. Many department stores and gas station stores have credit cards that you can only use at their store. Many of these stores will let kids sign up for a card if a parent *cosigns*. That means the parent also signs up on the account and is responsible if you don't pay back the money you borrow. These cards, too, can have high interest rates. They may also charge other fees.

COSIGN: to sign a legal document saying that you agree to pay someone else's debt if he or she does not pay it

Having a credit card can be a good way to build a history of good credit. Having good credit shows you can be trusted to borrow money for big purchases, like a car or a home, when you're older. But credit cards are not for everyone. It's important to spend only what you can afford to pay back. And it's important to pay it back as quickly as possible to avoid paying lots of interest.

DANGER: MINIMUM PAYMENT

Credit cards have a minimum payment that you have to make every month. The minimum might be really low, which is nice if you don't have much money to spare. The danger is that every month you don't pay off your whole balance, you get charged more interest. Say you buy a $50 sweater. The minimum payment next month is only $8. Great, you can afford that! But next month, your balance isn't $42 ($50 – $8). Instead, it's $46. That's because the credit card company charged you interest on the $42 balance. If you keep paying the minimum every month, it takes a long time to pay off your balance. That $50 sweater might end up costing $70 by the time you're done paying for it.

In addition to interest, you may have to pay an annual membership fee just to have the credit card.

If you think you're ready for this big responsibility, talk with your parent. For most kids, debit cards or prepaid cards are a good way to gain experience managing money without facing the temptation of a credit card. When you *are* ready to get a credit card, do your homework on the card you apply for. Find out what the repayment requirements are and how high the interest rate is. Ask an adult to help you choose the right card for you.

Choose Your Own Spending Ending
The Credit Card Dilemma

For your 13th birthday, your mom helps you sign up for a department store credit card. She cosigns, so if you don't pay back what you spend, it goes on her record. But she wants you to learn to manage credit. So she encourages you to make a few small purchases and pay them back the first month.

That weekend your mom takes you to the department store to buy a pair of Super Awesome Sneakers. While you're trying on the shoes, your mom heads off to look at jeans for your brother. The clerk rings up your new shoes, and it feels great to make the purchase all on your own.

As the clerk hands back your card, you notice a really neat pair of designer sunglasses. They're on display next to the cash register. *These would look great on Mom,* you think.

But your mom would never spend $129 on herself. Maybe it would be nice to buy them for her as a gift. After all, she does a lot of great things for you. And it's her birthday next week. You picture her smiling in these hot new shades. Every time she puts them on, she thinks of you. Before you know it, you're standing at the cash register again. You have the sunglasses in one hand and your new credit card in the other.

"Lovely choice," the cashier says. "Shall we put it on the card?"

"We shall," you say. But before she rings up the shades, you add up the sneakers and the sunglasses in your mind. They come out to more than $220 with tax. You've never even *seen* $220.

"Wait," you say. The cashier gives you an annoyed look.

What do you do?

1 › You picture your mom again, smiling and thanking you for the new shades. The wind blows in her hair, making her look like a movie star. It will feel so good to give her something she loves. "Never mind," you say. "I'll take them!" *Turn to* **Ending 1** *on page 116.*

* *

2 › You picture your mom again—and you remember her comparing the prices on two bicycle tires last summer. She chose the cheaper one even though she really wanted the nicer one. You think about how long it will take you to pay back $220 on the allowance you make. It would be a long time, especially with interest raising the total every month. "Sorry," you tell the cashier. "I changed my mind." You leave the sunglasses on the counter and walk out of the store. *Turn to* **Ending 2** *on page 117.*

* *

To sum up, here are the pros and cons of credit cards.

Pros

- You can build a credit history, showing future lenders that you're responsible.
- You get to enjoy a big purchase right away, even if you don't have enough cash to pay for it right now.

Cons

- You get to enjoy a big purchase right away, even if you don't have enough cash to pay for it right now. (Wait, this is a pro *and* a con? That's right. With a credit card, it's easy to get carried away and buy expensive things you really can't afford. You can end up with lots of credit card debt—when you owe a lot of money that takes you a long time to pay off.)
- If you don't pay off your balance every month, you have to pay interest. That can really add up.
- If you are late with a payment, many cards charge you a fee.

See Your Spending Ending
The Credit Card Dilemma

Ending 1

The cashier slides your credit card through the reader and hands it back to you with a big smile. "Your mother is going to love these," she says. She puts the shades in a fancy bag with a little colored tissue on top so it looks like a real gift. When you see your mom in the mall, you proudly hand it to her.

"Wow!" she says when she unwraps the sunglasses. "These are beautiful. But how did you afford them? They're really expensive."

"Don't worry about that, Mom," you say. It feels amazing to give her a gift she really loves.

But your mom does worry. When you admit that you bought them on the credit card, she makes you return them. You're disappointed at first, but then you realize it's the right thing to do. Even if you used *all* of your allowance to repay the loan, it would still take more than two years—especially because the interest would keep raising the balance. As it is, you'll be paying off your sneakers for a while.

The End

Ending 2

The cashier sneers, "Whatever."

She seems annoyed that you changed your mind, which is embarrassing. But you realize you can't afford the sunglasses. It would take you over two years to pay for them.

When your mom's birthday rolls around the next week, you make her a card like you always do. And she loves it—like she always does. You don't use the credit card any more while you're paying off your sneakers. You get a couple lawn-mowing jobs in your neighborhood so you can make bigger payments. Still, with interest, those $80 shoes end up costing about $105 by the time you pay them off.

The End

If you chose Ending 2, smart thinking! Of course, waiting to buy the shoes until you can afford to pay cash would be even smarter. By limiting credit card purchases, you avoid credit card debt, pay less interest, and have more money for saving. The next chapter has lots more information about saving.

8 Looking into Your Crystal Ball
(Saving and Investing)

It's time to look into the future. Grab your crystal ball and dim the lights. Gaze into the glowing ball. Concentrate. What do you see? Are you happy? Have your money smarts helped you feel safe and satisfied? Are you—

What's that? You don't have a crystal ball? Darn. That means you can't see into the future.

Oh, well. Neither can anyone else, actually. And since you can't predict the future, you will just have to do what all money-smart kids do: prepare. That means making goals and working hard to reach them. Most of all, it means saving. Put money aside and let it add up. It's not magic. It's math.

Remember those goals you started thinking about in Chapter 2? Some were long-term goals. Maybe you said you wanted to buy a jetpack and a hologram viewer and fly across the ocean while watching videos! Okay, you probably didn't say that. But maybe you *did* say you wanted to go to college or buy a car. Maybe you went really long-term, and really big, like buying a huge house in Hawaii. Saving is a super-important part of reaching goals like these. Even if you don't have any long-term goals yet, you will someday. So it's still wise to save.

You also want to save for emergencies. When you're a kid, your family will usually take care of you in an emergency. But as you get older, it's really smart to have some money saved up in case something big—and expensive—happens. Something like your car breaks down and you have to get it fixed. Or you lose your job and you need to pay your bills even though you don't have paychecks coming in. If you have enough saved up, you will be all right.

Start Early

A good way to start preparing for the future is to put money into a savings account, and you can start that now. Check out the section on savings accounts on pages 104–106. Ask at different banks to get the best interest rate available.

The sooner you start saving, the more money you'll have later in life. That's because the interest you earn has longer to accumulate. There are two kinds of interest: simple interest and compound interest.

Simple Interest

Simple interest is calculated only on the amount of money you originally deposit, and it is calculated annually. So if you put $200 in a savings account and the interest rate is 1 percent, then you will make $2 a year in interest ($200 x 0.01 = $2). Your total balance is then $202. If you leave the money in there for two years, you'll earn $4. That brings your balance to $204.

Pretty simple, right? That's why they call it simple interest. Compound interest, which banks use much more often, is a little more complicated.

Compound Interest

Compound interest is much better for you than simple interest, and it is the key to saving for your future. Compound interest is calculated not only on the money you originally deposited, but also on any interest the money in your account has already earned. Most savings accounts pay compound interest, and most compound annually. That means that once a year, they add the interest you made that year onto your total. Then the following year, you are earning interest on the new total, not just your original deposit.

Looking at the previous example, if you invest $200 in an account that earns 1 percent interest compounded annually, the first year will be the same. You'll end up earning $2, bringing your total up to $202. But the second year, you earn interest on $202, not just on $200, so $202 x 0.01 = 2.02. So you make two extra cents that year, and now your total is $204.02.

$200.00	original deposit
2.00	interest first year
2.02	interest second year
$204.02	total after two years

That might not seem like a big difference after two years. But if you keep adding to your *principal*, the balance gets even higher. And then you earn even more interest. The more money you have in the account, the more money you earn. Keep adding, and keep earning. Adding a little bit now and a little bit later— and continuing to add—will make a big difference in the long run.

PRINCIPAL: the amount of money you invest in an account, separate from the interest you earn

Investing is a way for you to save and earn even more money. You'll read more about investing on pages 123–132. But first, imagine yourself in the following story and choose a spending ending.

Choose Your Own Spending Ending

Invest Your Best

Your grandmother gives you $50 for your birthday, doubling the savings you already have. You don't really have any solid long-term goals yet—other than having a lot of money one day. But with the 1 percent you earn on your savings account, you feel like you'll never get there. And you thought compound interest was supposed to be so great.

Instead of saving, you give up. "Thanks for the money, Grandma. I think I'll buy enough gumballs to fill the kiddie pool for my birthday party."

"I thought you were going to save it," your grandmother says.

"I was," you say. But then you explain how long it would take to earn any real money. "So I might as well have some fun now."

"Just a second," your grandmother says. "You don't just put the $100 in there and forget about it. You keep adding to it, so it will grow faster. Plus, if you are interested, I can help you invest some of that money so it grows even faster."

"What do you mean, *invest?*"

"You can put that money in some other accounts besides a regular savings account. These other accounts might earn you some more money."

What do you do?

1 › You prefer to buy a pool full of gumballs and have a party with your friends. Your grandmother said the investments *might* help you save money, and that doesn't sound very reassuring. Saving money is a rip-off! *Turn to* **Ending 1** *on page 129.*

2 › You listen to your grandmother describe some of the options for investing. And you decide to give her way a chance. *Turn to* **Ending 2** *on page 129.*

Investing Your Money

Investing can earn you more money than a regular savings account. But investments are long-term. When you put money into an investment, you typically won't see your earnings until years in the future. And with some investments, there's a chance you could lose some or all of your money.

When considering an investment, here are three factors to look at:

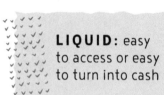

- **Safety:** What are the chances that you will lose money instead of earn it?

- **Access:** How easily can you get your money out of the investment? Another way to ask this question is: How *liquid* is your money?

  LIQUID: easy to access or easy to turn into cash

- **Return on investment (ROI):** How much money can you earn on the investment?

For the most part, the riskier the investment, the more you might be able to earn. Safer investments don't offer as much reward, but they are, you know, *safer*.

Here are the types of investments you should be aware of.

Certificates of Deposit

These are also known as CDs. In some ways, they are like savings accounts. You deposit money in the bank and earn interest on it. But you are usually expected to keep your money in the bank for a fixed amount of time without making any withdrawals. In exchange, the bank will give you a slightly higher interest rate than it would for a savings account. When you buy a CD, the bank gives you a certificate stating the amount you invested.

Let's rate the safety, ease of access, and ROI for certificates of deposit on a scale of 1 to 5 stars. Five stars is the best rating.

- **Safety:** ★ ★ ★ ★ ★ The bank insures your CD, so the money is protected, making it very safe.
- **Access:** ★ You are not free to take the money out whenever you want, so it's not very liquid.
- **ROI:** ★ ★ The ROI is better than your savings account's ROI because the interest rate is higher.

Money Market Accounts

Also known as MMAs, these are also similar to savings accounts, but they usually offer higher interest rates. They also usually require a high minimum balance.

- **Safety:** ★ ★ ★ ★ ★ Like CDs, MMAs are insured, so they are a safe investment.
- **Access:** ★ ★ ★ ★ MMAs are more liquid than CDs because you can take money out whenever you want. But there is usually a minimum balance you have to keep up.
- **ROI:** ★ ★ ★ The more money you keep in the MMA, the more interest you can earn.

Bonds

When you buy U.S. bonds, you're lending money to the national government. The government pays it back, with interest, when you cash it in. The United States first started selling bonds during World Wars I and II to help pay for fighting the wars. But they are still used today.

- **Safety:** ★ ★ ★ ★ ★ Bonds are guaranteed by the U.S. government, making them a very safe investment option.
- **Access:** ★ ★ ★ ★ ★ A bond *can* be as liquid as you want, but they are meant to be held onto for years while they earn interest.

- ROI: ★ ★ Because bonds are so safe, the interest rate is not very high.

Stocks

A stock is a share of a company. When you buy stock, you become a part owner of that company—a very small part. You don't have any say in how the company does business (unless you own a *lot* of stock). But you do get to enjoy part of the company's earnings. If the company does well, then the value of its stock goes up. If the company does poorly, the value of the stock goes down.

For example, say you buy 10 shares of stock in the Super Awesome Sneakers company. Each share costs $10, so your 10 shares cost $100 ($10 x 10 shares = $100). And let's say lots of people buy Super Awesome Sneakers, and the company's owners run it well. The value of each share might go up. Six months later, each share might be worth $12. Now those 10 shares you paid $100 for are worth $120.

- Safety: ★ ★ Stocks are a much riskier investment than CDs, MMAs, and bonds because they are not insured. You are basically gambling that the company will improve its value over time.

- Access: ★ ★ ★ ★ ★ You can sell your stocks at any time, so they are liquid. But when you sell, you sell for the value of the stock at that time. If the value has gone up, then you make money. If it has gone down, you lose money.

- ROI: ★ ★ ★ ★ ★ Stocks can quickly rise or drop in value, so the ROI can be unpredictable. Most of the time, companies are fairly stable and their value goes up slowly but steadily. But there are no guarantees.

Grace Under Pressure

My name is Grace, and when I turned 14, I got a job at an ice cream parlor. When I got my first paycheck, I was a little disappointed. My check was only for $86.56. After I donated $20 to a charity that helps homeless kids, I was down to $66.56.

I realized that it would take me a very long time to save up much money. When my older brother heard me grumbling, he showed me a video about investments. He was studying investing as a way to save more money. Watching that video, I got excited.

The video showed me how to research stocks online. First I look to see if the company has good management and if its stock has grown in value over time. The first stock I bought (with my parents' help) was shares of the ice cream parlor where I worked. Almost right away, the stock started to go down in value! The value went down for about a week, but I tried not to panic. That's something else I learned in the video. Stocks are long-term investments, so you have to be patient. Even though it made me sick to see my investment dwindling, I waited it out. And guess what? Pretty soon the stock began to go back up again. It's almost up to what I paid for it now, and I expect it to keep going up.

Since then I have invested in more stock. But I always research every company online before investing. I expect to earn money steadily over time—using patience and research. My stock investments will help me pay for college.

Mutual Funds

Some investors combine their money with other investors' money in one big fund—called a mutual fund—to buy many kinds of investments, like stocks, bonds, and MMAs. Someone manages the fund. The fund manager trades the fund's different investments to try to earn a profit and collect interest.

- Safety: ★ ★ ★ Mutual funds are not insured, making them less safe than bonds, MMAs, and CDs. But they are managed by experts. Fund managers usually have lots of experience, which helps them make smart decisions and earn money for everyone who invests in the mutual fund. And mutual funds are *diversified*, which also helps make them safer.

- Access: ★ ★ ★ ★ You are free to withdraw your money from a mutual fund at any time. When you withdraw, your shares are worth what they are

DIVERSIFY: to put your investment money into several different types of investments. When investments are diversified, the overall risk is lower.

worth that day—not when you bought in. The value of your shares may be higher or lower than when you paid for them.

- **ROI:** ★ ★ ★ Like stocks, mutual funds can go up and down in value, so the ROI can be unpredictable, too. But unlike stocks, mutual funds have a fund manager, who is an expert at getting the best return on an investment.

Collectibles

Collectibles are just what they sound like—things you collect. You buy them and hold onto them for a long time, hoping that their value increases. Then you sell them. People collect stamps, coins, comic books, action figures, art, and many other things.

- **Safety:** ★ ★ There is no guarantee that collectibles will go up in value. There is also no guarantee you'll be able to find someone who is willing to buy them. So collectibles are a risky investment.

- **Access:** ★ Collectibles are not very liquid. The only way to get your money back is to find someone who wants to buy them. If you can't, then you keep holding onto the items.

- **ROI:** ★ ★ Collectibles tend to gain value slowly. You may have to hold onto them for many years before you can make money selling them.

See Your Spending Ending
Invest Your Best

Ending 1

"Sorry, Grandma," you say. "I'm just a kid, and I don't feel like stashing all my money away and waiting for a million years. I want to have fun!"

You order 60 gallons of gumballs and get your kiddie pool ready. You call up your two best buddies, and you host the greatest gumball birthday party ever! As you jump into the pool and chew wads of gum, you are so excited you let out a big *whooooop!* That night, your friends sleep over, and you sit in the gumball pool while playing video games and watching movies you rented—and chewing lots of gum, of course. Everyone gets sick to their stomachs, goes to bed, and wakes up with gum in their hair. But you all agree it was worth it and you would do it again in a heartbeat.

While you're doing laundry to get the chewed gum out of your bedsheets, your grandmother comes over to visit. "How much money do you have left?" she asks.

You're not actually sure, so you go to your wallet and count it up: $9.48.

"Well, I'm glad you had a happy birthday," your grandmother says.

You're glad, too. But looking into that nearly empty wallet, you think about how full it was yesterday. It makes you almost as sick as all that gum did.

The End

. . . .

Ending 2

"Let's give it a shot," you say.

"You got it," your grandmother says. She opens up her laptop and shows you the CDs, bonds, and mutual funds she owns. You could buy into any of those—or all of them. She recommends putting about half of the money into a CD. She has one CD that you have to keep your money in for five years, with an interest rate of 2.25 percent. You decide to put $50 into that CD. When you take the money out in five years, it will have grown to be more than $55.

You invest $25 in some of the stocks your grandmother owns, too. Over the next few months, the two of you get together several times and check to see how they are doing. It's a fun way for the two of you to spend time together. Even better—the stocks do well! You invest more gift money into your stocks after every birthday. Within five years, you have about $250 worth of stock. You decide to sell some of it. Then you combine that profit with the $55 from your CD, and you put all that into another, bigger CD.

For your birthday, you do not have a gumball pool party. But you do invite your buddies over to spend the night. Your grandmother makes root beer floats, and you stay up way too late watching movies. It's not quite as amazing as the gumball pool party would have been. But you have a fun time, and you feel great that you're investing in your future.

The End

Choosing the Right Investments for You

Because investments involve risk, you can lose some or all of your money. To protect against that, people diversify their investments. That means they divide their money among several different kinds of investments. This is the idea behind mutual funds (see pages 127–128). But you can diversify all your investments. A smart investor will have money in savings accounts, CDs, bonds, stocks, *and* mutual funds. That way you take on *some* risk with the hope that the risk pays off in higher ROIs. Meanwhile, the safer investments keep you from losing too much.

Take a look at the mountain below. It shows the risks and rewards of different kinds of investments. Investments with lower risks and lower returns are at the bottom of the mountain. The bottom is a large, stable base. As you move up the mountain, returns usually become greater, but so do the risks. Only put your money in investments higher on the mountain after you have built a strong base.

And only put your money into investments higher up the mountain if you feel comfortable taking some risk. Remember, you are not guaranteed to make money. The higher ROIs you can get at the top are tempting, but they can end up costing you.

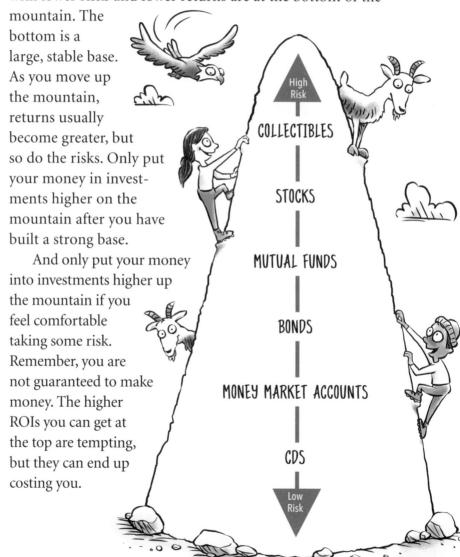

High
Risk

COLLECTIBLES

STOCKS

MUTUAL FUNDS

BONDS

MONEY MARKET ACCOUNTS

CDS

Low
Risk

A good way to learn about investing is to create a fantasy account of $10,000 and pretend you're putting that money into different investments. Then track how those investments do for a year. You can find the value of most types of investments online. An adult can help you if you have trouble finding certain information.

Here's an example of what a fantasy account might look like. (See page 135 for a blank chart you can use to keep track of your own fantasy account.)

My Fantasy Investments

Name of Investment	Amount Invested	After 3 Months	After 6 Months	After 9 Months	After 12 Months	Amount Made or Lost
CD from Bank A	$2,000	$2,005	$2,011	$2,016	$2,022	+$22
Stock B	$4,000	$4,160	$4,112	$4,189	$3,923	-$77
Stock C	$4,000	$4,370	$4,320	$4,380	$4,402	+$402
Total Made or Lost						+$347

A Money–Smart Future

You've learned a lot of skills, tips, and information in this book. You've learned how to use financial tools from budgets to credit cards. You've read about how to be thoughtful and mindful about spending money, and you've learned how to invest wisely.

As you can see, a lot goes into being money smart. Right now, you're a kid, and chances are you don't have a credit card and you don't get paychecks. It's likely that you haven't invested in stocks or CDs yet. And you probably do not have a

Saving for College

Everyone knows that college can be very costly. Some schools charge more than $60,000 a year! But did you also know that there are special plans just for saving for college? They are officially called 529 plans, but many people just call them "college savings plans." These plans let you, your parents or guardians, and anyone else (grandparents, for instance) save money for your college costs in the future. A big benefit of 529 plans is that you don't pay taxes when you use the money for college costs. But a drawback is that the plans may have high fees that can wipe out what you save by not paying taxes. If you and your parents or guardians are thinking about opening a 529 plan, talk to a financial expert first.

To find out more about 529 plans, type the name of your state and "529 plan" into an online search engine.

whole bunch of money. But you don't *need* a bunch of money to start being money smart. The point of this book isn't to make you rich. It's to help guide you in the important financial decisions you'll make throughout your life—from goal setting, to earning, to spending, donating, and saving (and investing). These decisions will reflect who you are as a person.

When you're money smart, you make decisions that make you feel proud, secure, and happy. One challenge will be resisting the many temptations we all face to spend (or waste) our money. You want to be careful and thoughtful. Remember: It's okay to spend money on a treat for yourself every now and then. If a new book, game, or T-shirt will make you happy, guess what? Happiness is important! As long as you don't constantly buy yourself treats and never save anything, then you'll be okay. And you'll probably be happier in the long run.

Having money smarts is all about keeping one eye on the future. You can have fun and be smart all at the same time. And who doesn't want to be fun and smart?

Track Your Fantasy Investments

To get some practice thinking about investing, try "fantasy investing." Pick several types of investments—CDs, MMAs, bonds, mutual funds, stocks, or even a collectible. Write down the investments you pick in the first column and how much you invest in each in the second column. Write today's date as the starting date.

Then, every three months, note how much your fantasy investments are worth. Ideally, you'll do this for a whole year—because just like real investments, your fantasy investments are meant to be a long-term commitment. You should be able to look up your investments' value online. If you have trouble finding the right information, you can ask an adult to help you.

At the end of the year, calculate whether your fantasy investments went up in value and you made money, or whether they went down in value and you lost money. (See page 132 for an example of how to complete this chart. You can also use this chart to track real investments.)

Starting Date: _____

Name of Investment	Amount Invested	After 3 Months	After 6 Months	After 9 Months	After 12 Months	Amount Made or Lost
Total Made or Lost						

Glossary

advertise: to let people know about a product or business

allowance: an amount of money given to someone on a regular basis

balance: the amount of money in an account

boycott: to refuse to buy or use something as a way to protest how a company does business

charity: an organization that raises money to help people, animals, or the environment, or to address other needs

check: a written note that tells your bank to pay money from your account. When you have a checking account, the bank gives you a book full of checks with your account number on them. You fill out the checks with information about specific payments.

consequence: the result of an action

consistent: not changing; done the same way every time

consumer: someone who buys goods and services

cosign: to sign a legal document saying that you agree to pay someone else's debt if he or she does not pay it

currency: the type of money used in a specific country

debit card: a plastic card that is issued by a bank and that you can use to buy things. The money you spend is taken out of your bank account at the time of the purchase.

debt: money owed to a person or an institution, such as a bank

deliberate: thoughtful, careful, and planned

diversify: to put your investment money into several different types of investments. When investments are diversified, the overall risk is lower.

donate: to give money away to a good cause

ethical: trying to do the right thing; morally right or good

exchange: to trade one thing for another (such as money for goods)

expenses: money you spend to run your business

fee: a payment for a service

financial: having to do with money

impulsive: doing something based on a sudden urge and without thinking about it

income tax: a percentage of your income that you must pay to the government

interest: the charge on borrowed money

labor: work someone does for pay

landfill: an area where waste is buried in the ground, potentially poisoning the land and water, or releasing greenhouse gasses that affect climate change

liquid: easy to access or easy to turn into cash

overhead: money that a business or organization spends on things that keep it running, such as salaries or rent

password: a word, set of numbers, or combination of letters and numbers that you keep secret and use to access something private, such as a bank account

peer pressure: influence from your friends urging you to think or act a certain way

principal: the amount of money you invest in an account, separate from the interest you earn

prioritize: to rank things in order of importance

profit: money you make after expenses

sales tax: a percentage of the price of a purchased item, which goes to the government

secure: feeling safe, sure of yourself, and confident about the future

sustainability: the act of producing goods in a way that does as little harm to the environment and to communities as possible

unbiased: having a fair opinion about something without favoring one point of view

values: ideas and principles that are important to you

Resources

Charity Navigator
charitynavigator.org
Use this site to help find charities that match your values
and that spend donations wisely.

Get a Job Helping Others by Ryan Jacobsen (Minneapolis:
Lerner Publications, 2015). Learn about some of the jobs
you can take on in your neighborhood, such as mowing
lawns, walking dogs, tutoring, and others.

The Good Shopping Guide
thegoodshoppingguide.com
This organization compares the ethics of companies
worldwide so you can easily see how they are using
consumers' money to impact the world. Use this resource
to make more mindful spending decisions.

Kids Health: School & Jobs
kidshealth.org/en/teens/school-jobs
This site for teens has a section labeled "Jobs & Volunteering"
where visitors can read a dozen articles about interviews, job
hunting, babysitting resources, and lots more.

*National Geographic Kids Everything Money: A Wealth of
Facts, Photos, and Fun!* by Kathy Furgang (Washington, DC:
National Geographic Children's Books, 2013). This book
offers a fun look at money, including its history and myths,
as well as help with saving and spending.

PBS Kids It's My Life: Managing Money
pbskids.org/itsmylife/money/managing
Learn about spending and saving, money goals, using budgets, and more.

What Color Is Your Parachute? For Teens by Carol Christen (New York: Ten Speed Press, 2015). This career guide for kids ages 12 and up helps you figure out what you're good at, what you love, and what you might want to be.

What Do You Really Want? How to Set a Goal and Go for It! A Guide for Teens (Revised & Updated) by Beverly K. Bachel (Minneapolis: Free Spirit Publishing, 2016). For ages 11 and up, this guide helps you figure out your goals, set priorities and deadlines, overcome obstacles, build a support system, use positive self-talk, celebrate successes, and more.

Index

Other Great Books from Free Spirit

The Survival Guide
for School Success
*Ron Shumsky, Susan M.
Islascox, and Rob Bell*
For ages 10–14.

The Survival Guide
for Making and
Being Friends
James J. Crist, Ph.D.
For ages 8–13.

The Survival Guide for Kids
with Behavior Challenges
Tom McIntyre, Ph.D.
For ages 9–14.

The Survival Guide
for Gifted Kids
Judy Galbraith
For ages 10 & under.

The Survival Guide
for Kids with ADHD
John F. Taylor, Ph.D.
For ages 8–12.

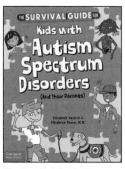

The Survival Guide for
Kids with Autism Spectrum
Disorders (And Their Parents)
*Elizabeth Verdick and Elizabeth
Reeve, M.D.*
For ages 9–13.

The Survival Guide
for Kids with LD
Rhoda Cummings, Ed.D.
For ages 8–13.

The Survival Guide
for Kids with Physical
Disabilities & Challenges
*Wendy L. Moss, Ph.D., and
Susan A. Taddonio, D.P.T.*
For ages 8–13.

Find all the Free Spirit SURVIVAL GUIDES for Kids at www.freespirit.com/survival-guides-for-kids

For pricing information, to place an order, or to request a free catalog, contact:
Free Spirit Publishing Inc.
6325 Sandburg Road • Suite 100 • Minneapolis, MN 55427-3674 • toll-free 800.735.7323
local 612.338.2068 • fax 612.337.5050 • help4kids@freespirit.com • www.freespirit.com

About the Authors

Eric Braun is a writer, editor, bicyclist, punk music connoisseur, and serious baseball fan. He writes fiction and nonfiction books for kids and adults, and he has won a McKnight Fellowship and other awards and honors for his writing. He has an MFA in creative writing and a bachelor's degree in English. He lives in Minneapolis with his wife—who wrote this book with him—and his two sons—who inspired the idea for the book.

Sandy Donovan writes for kids and adults. For kids, she writes books about money and economics, history, science, and sometimes pop stars. For adults, she writes about career planning, education, and jobs. When she's not writing, she's usually reading magazines, running, watching her sons play baseball, or working at her job as a policy analyst and website developer for the U.S. Department of Labor. She has a master's degree in public policy and a bachelor's degree in journalism.

About the Illustrator

Steve Mark is a freelance illustrator and a part-time puppeteer. He lives in Minnesota and is the father of three and the husband of one. Steve has illustrated several books in the Laugh & Learn series, including *Bullying Is a Pain in the Brain, Don't Behave Like You Live in a Cave, Stand Up to Bullying!*, and *Siblings: You're Stuck with Each Other, So Stick Together.*